A Cut Above

Turn Charm Squares, Strips, and More into Beautiful Patchwork

GERRI ROBINSON

Martingale
Create with Confidence

Dedication

To my immediate and extended family: thank you for your support and belief in my work. Your encouragement inspires me to keep going and push myself and my creative boundaries daily.

A Cut Above: Turn Charm Squares, Strips, and More into Beautiful Patchwork

© 2013 by Gerri Robinson

Martingale®
19021 120th Ave. NE, Ste. 102
Bothell, WA 98011-9511 USA
ShopMartingale.com

Printed in China
18 17 16 15 14 13   8 7 6 5 4 3 2 1

Library of Congress Cataloging-in-Publication Data is available upon request.

ISBN: 978-1-60468-357-8

Mission Statement
Dedicated to providing quality products and service to inspire creativity.

Credits
PRESIDENT AND CEO: Tom Wierzbicki
EDITOR IN CHIEF: Mary V. Green
DESIGN DIRECTOR: Paula Schlosser
MANAGING EDITOR: Karen Costello Soltys
ACQUISITIONS EDITOR: Karen M. Burns
TECHNICAL EDITOR: Nancy Mahoney
COPY EDITOR: Marcy Heffernan
PRODUCTION MANAGER: Regina Girard
COVER AND INTERIOR DESIGNERS: Paula Schlosser
    and Connor Chin
PHOTOGRAPHER: Brent Kane
ILLUSTRATOR: Rose Wright

Special thanks to Kim Thomas and Joe Zapalac and their two sons Travis and Wyatt as well as Sheila and Jonathan Waterman and their two kids Madison and Olivia for generously allowing us to photograph in their home.

Contents

Introduction

I never fully embraced the quilting industry's lineup of precut fabric collections until the spring of 2012. I know, I was a little late joining the party, but I'm so glad I did.

Why did it take me so long? I really don't have a definitive answer, but I'm sure it's at least partly due to the fact that I had a "limited" understanding of the concept. My thought was why *limit* yourself to 2½", 5", and 10" squares, or 2½"-wide strips, or fat eighths (9" x 21" rectangles), or even fat quarters (18" x 21") when you can have an endless supply of fabric and a creative platform with continuous yardage? I was limiting myself by my own thinking—never a good idea.

Did my thinking evolve after watching numerous seasons of *Project Runway,* where designers are faced weekly with some pretty incredible challenges and in turn create some pretty spectacular fashion collections? Or was the timing just right for me to step outside my comfort zone and challenge myself? I believe all things are a combination of many elements and events.

The designs found throughout the pages of *A Cut Above* chronicle the steps I took to overcome my own design obstacles about working in a precut environment. With all new things, it's best to start small, so I began with 2½" squares. I could feel my confidence building, so I moved on to my next challenge: 5" and 10" squares. Momentum built, and the next thing I knew, 2½"-wide strips, fat eighths, and fat quarters were no longer an obstacle, but rather staples of my design thinking and creativity. Eventually, I even coined some new terms—2½" *itty bits* and 5" *little bits of charm.*

I used this same sequence to lay out the projects in this book: 2½", 5", and 10" squares; 2½"-wide strips; fat eighths; and fat quarters. Did you realize you can create a 90"-square queen-size bed quilt from 10" squares? I'll show you how in my "Dancing among the Stars" quilt on page 35.

Grab some fat eighths and you're on your way to making a pretty amazing quilt. "Summer Time" on page 54 has enough fabric left over to create a companion quilt, "A 'Digital' Trip around the World" on page 58. Now, that's a cut above—two quilts from 9" x 21" pieces of fabric! Raise a glass to that . . . cheers!

To offer you variety and flexibility, I'll show you how a design can change before your eyes, either by controlling the exact placement of the fabrics in each block for a planned design or throwing caution to the wind and letting the fabrics fall where they may to create a fantastic scrappy look. It's amazing how changing fabric placement can affect the look and feel of a design. Check out "Buttoned Up" on page 40 and "Carefree" on page 43 to see what I mean.

As a special surprise to me, and an added bonus for you, "Rugby Stars" on page 62 generated quite a few trimmed-corner leftovers, which I used to create "Board Game" on page 67 and its coordinating companion pillows. There were enough 2½"-wide strips leftover after making "Friendship" on page 29 to create a companion framed wall hanging, "Do-Si-Do" on page 32.

If you're already fond of precuts, I hope the designs inspire you to keep using them. If you're new to the party like me, peruse the pages, but don't wait too long—precuts are waiting for you to enjoy!

Working with Precuts

Precuts are packaged bundles of fabric cut to specific sizes, such as 5" squares or 2½"-wide strips. You can use manufactured precuts or make your own. How about both? The quilts in this book were designed primarily from Moda's vast assortment of precuts, but I created "Galaxy" on page 26 from my fabric remnants.

Turning Fabric Leftovers into Precuts

I challenge you to look at your end-of-project remnants or fabric leftovers differently. Instead of folding the various sizes of your fabric pieces and putting them back into your fabric stash, begin to cut your remnants into various sizes and sort them by like colors—reds, greens, blues, browns; or theme categories such as backgrounds, bright colors, Civil War reproductions, and so forth. You might surprise yourself how quickly a color assortment or theme comes together.

To Trim or Not to Trim

A great debate? Not for me. I don't trim the pinked edges from any of the industry precuts. Simply line up the outer points of the pinked edges to the cutting line and cut your precut squares into the desired sizes. (When stitching, sew ¼" from the outer points as well.)

Quiltmaking Basics

All of the quilts in *A Cut Above* are made using basic quilting techniques. On the following pages, you'll find my methods for making:

- Flying-geese units
- Half-square-triangle units
- Quick-angled rectangles
- Square-in-a-square units
- Pieced sashing
- Wool appliqué

There are numerous ways of doing these techniques. The use of special rulers and tools really expands your options, but for the sake of simplicity, my instructions are for "old school" techniques—no special rulers or papers—just the basics. All you'll need is a self-healing cutting mat, an acrylic ruler, a rotary cutter, and fabric.

Flying-Geese Units

Draw a diagonal line on the wrong side of two 2½" squares. Place a marked square on one end of a 2½" x 4½" rectangle, right sides together. Sew on the drawn line. Trim the excess corner fabric, leaving a ¼" seam allowance and press the resulting triangle open. Repeat the process on the other end of the rectangle to complete a flying-geese unit.

Half-Square-Triangle Units

Draw a diagonal line on the wrong side of a 2⅞" square. Layer the marked square right sides together with a second 2⅞" square. Sew ¼" on each side of the marked line. Cut the squares apart on the marked line and press the seam allowances toward the darker triangle.

Quick-Angled Rectangles

Draw a diagonal line on the wrong side of a 2½" square. Place the marked square on one end of a 2½" x 4½" rectangle, right sides together. Sew on the drawn line. Trim the excess corner fabric, leaving a ¼" seam allowance and press the resulting triangle open.

Square-in-a-Square Units

Draw a diagonal line on the wrong side of a 2½" square. Place the marked square on one corner of a 4½" square. Sew on the drawn line. Trim the excess corner fabric, leaving a ¼" seam allowance and press the resulting triangle open. Repeat the process to sew marked squares on the three remaining corners of the larger square.

Pieced Sashing

Draw a diagonal line on the wrong side of two 1½" squares. Place a marked square on one corner of a 2½" x 8½" rectangle, right sides together. Sew on the drawn line. Trim the excess corner fabric, leaving a ¼" seam allowance and press the resulting triangle open. Repeat the process, sewing a marked square on the adjacent corner of the rectangle as shown.

 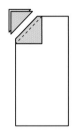 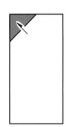 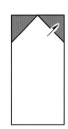

Wool Appliqué

I feel I should write a blinking disclaimer for this section because of the raw nature of my approach. For those who know me, I love and admire appliqué on quilts and I have attempted it on several of my own designs, including "Wild Rose Mini Sampler" on page 18. But for me, it's a slow and methodical process and I typically don't have time due to my schedule and deadlines.

However, because of the finishing touch appliqué adds to a quilt (and sometimes a quilt just needs a little bit of appliqué to bring the design together), I'm sharing my own personal method of appliqué. A friend of mine best describes my approach as "Rebecc-liqué." I know you're now either interested or scared.

For me, wool appliqué is best because I don't have to think about the right or wrong side of the fabric. All sides are created equal—or at least I treat them equally.

Simply trace the appliqué design onto paper and cut out the shape on the drawn line. Pin the appliqué shape onto your wool and cut around the paper.

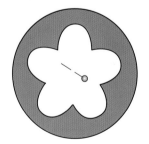 

Place the wool-appliqué piece onto the background fabric. Once you're satisfied with the placement, dab small dots of fabric glue around the perimeter on the underside of the shape to hold it in place. The stitching around the appliqué shape, to hold it in place, occurs during the quilting process. Simply stitch very close to the outer edge of the appliqué, around the entire shape. Let your creativity go and add quilting details to bring each element to life, like my long-arm quilter, Rebecca, does oh so effortlessly; hence the technique name "Rebecc-liqué."

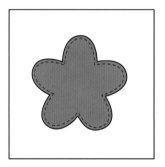

Framing Quilts

Several of the quilts in *A Cut Above* are framed. I took the guidance and suggestions of my local frame shop in preparing my quilts for framing. Here are their recommendations:

- Add a 2"-wide border to the pieced top. It's *not* necessary to match or coordinate the border to the quilt top since the border will be pulled and pinned to the back of an acid-free board prior to framing.
- Layer the quilt top with batting and backing; quilt as desired, leaving the 2"-wide outer border *unquilted*. Once the quilting is completed, fold the outer border toward the center of the quilt and carefully trim the backing and batting ¼" inside the quilt top edge. *Do not* bind your quilt.
- Lay the frame front side down on a table. Lay the quilt over the frame, ensuring the block is straight. Add the back of the frame and slide the frame clips in place. You may choose to finish your framed quilt with a glass front. For the designs in this book, I chose not to add glass to my framed quilts.

Adding Borders

The process for adding a border is the same whether it's an inner or outer border. For the quilts in this book, all of the inner-border strips are cut across the width of the fabric and pieced to their desired lengths as needed. Unless instructed otherwise, all of the outer-border strips are cut from the lengthwise grain of the fabric.

To determine the length to cut the side borders, measure the length of the quilt top through the middle. Cut two strips the length of that measurement. Mark the center of the quilt edges and the border strips. Pin the borders to the sides of the quilt top, matching the centers and ends. Sew the borders in place, easing as necessary. Press the seam allowances toward the border strips.

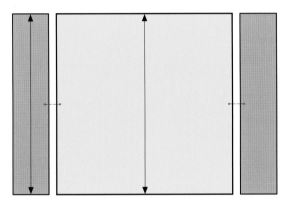

Measure the width of the quilt top through the middle, including the side borders just added. Cut two border strips to that measurement. Mark and pin the borders to the top and bottom of your quilt; then sew them as described for the side borders. Press the seam allowances toward the border strips.

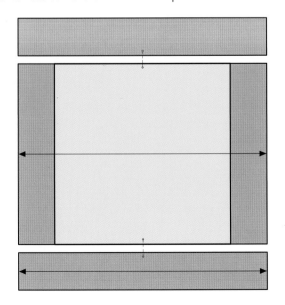

Layering and Quilting

All the quilts in *A Cut Above* were quilted using a long-arm quilting machine. Most professional quilters prefer an additional 5" of batting and backing all around the perimeter of the quilt. This additional amount of the backing fabric is included in the yardage requirements for each quilt. If you plan to have your quilt professionally machine quilted, be sure to check with the quilter regarding the backing size and preparation of your quilt top.

For free, downloadable, illustrated instructions on layering, basting, and quilting your quilt top, go to ShopMartingale.com/HowtoQuilt.

Binding

The preference of a fully machine-stitched or hand-sewn binding is truly a personal one. My preference is machine sewn, front and back, purely for the sake of saving time. If your quilt is going to be judged, I recommend hand sewing your binding to the quilt back in the final step.

For the binding, I cut strips 2½"-wide across the width of the fabric; the instructions for each quilt will tell you how many strips are required.

1 Join strips at right angles, right sides together, and stitch across the corner as shown. Trim the excess fabric, leaving a ¼" seam allowance. Press the seam allowances open.

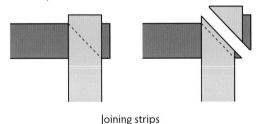

Joining strips

2 Fold the strip in half lengthwise, wrong sides together, and press.

Fold line

3 Trim the batting and backing even with the quilt top.

4 Starting on one side and beginning 8" from the end of the strip, use a ¼"-wide seam allowance to sew the binding strip to the quilt. Stop ¼" from the first corner and backstitch.

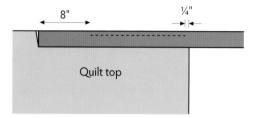

5 Turn the quilt so you'll be stitching down the next side. Fold the binding straight up and away from the quilt so the fold forms a 45° angle. Fold the binding back down on itself, even with the edge of the quilt top. Begin with a backstitch at the fold of the binding and continue stitching along the edge of the quilt top, mitering each corner as you come to it.

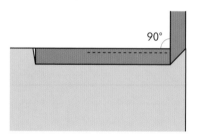

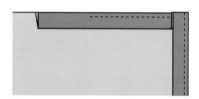

6 On the last side of the quilt, stop stitching 12" from where you began and backstitch. Remove the quilt from the machine. Overlap the binding ending tail with the starting tail. Trim the binding ends with a perpendicular cut so that the overlap is exactly 2½" (or the width you cut your binding).

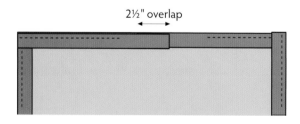

2½" overlap

7 Place the binding ends together at right angles. Mark a diagonal line and sew as shown. Trim, leaving a ¼" seam allowance. Press the seam allowances open. Reposition the binding on the quilt and finish sewing.

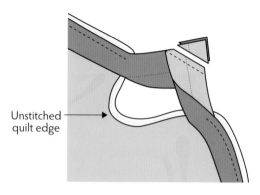

Unstitched quilt edge

8 Fold the binding to the back of the quilt, with the folded edge covering the row of machine stitching. Hand or machine stitch in place, mitering the corners.

Quilt back

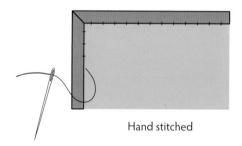

Hand stitched

Machine stitched

Itty-Bits and
Little Bits of Charm

Discover the charm of creating small wonders of art with
2½" and 5" squares of fabric. Let the designs stand alone, or
use them as the centerpiece in a larger and grander design.

Trail of Stars

An assortment of precut 2½" squares come together quite quickly and easily, creating a trail of stars suitable for framing.

Materials

Yardage is based on 42"-wide fabric unless otherwise noted.

36 squares, 2½" x 2½", of assorted dark and medium prints for Star blocks

¼ yard of cream solid for block background

¼ yard of fabric for framing or binding

½ yard of fabric for backing

18" x 34" piece of batting

Cutting

From the cream solid, cut:

12 rectangles, 2½" x 4½"

12 squares, 2½" x 2½"

From the framing or binding fabric, cut:*

2 border strips, 2" x 42"

*For binding, cut 2 strips, 2½" x 42"

TECHNIQUE USED

• Flying-Geese Units (page 7)

Making the Star Blocks

1 Sew four assorted 2½" squares together to make a four-patch unit. Press the seam allowances in the directions indicated. The unit should measure 4½" square. Make a total of three units.

Make 3.

2 Use two assorted 2½" squares and one cream 2½" x 4½" rectangle to make a flying-geese unit. The unit should measure 2½" x 4½". Make a total of 12 units.

Make 12.

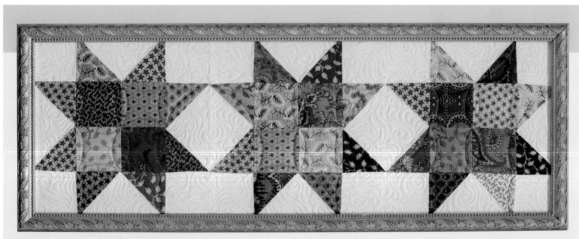

Designed and pieced by Gerri Robinson.
Machine quilted by Rebecca Segura.

FINISHED QUILT: 24" x 8"   **FINISHED BLOCK:** 8" x 8"

3 Sew two flying-geese units from step 2 to opposite sides of a four-patch unit as shown to make a center unit. Press the seam allowances toward the center. The unit should measure 4½" x 8½". Make a total of three units.

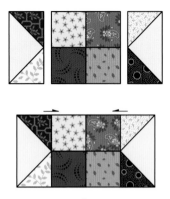

Make 3.

4 Sew a cream 2½" square to each end of the remaining flying-geese units to make 2½" x 8½" strips. Press the seam allowances toward the cream squares. Make a total of six strips.

Make 6.

5 Sew two pieced strips from step 4 and one center unit from step 3 together to complete a Star block. Press the seam allowances toward the center. The block should measure 8½" square. Make a total of three blocks.

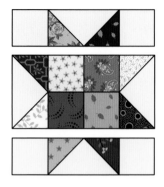

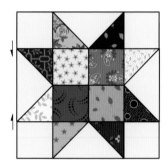

Make 3.

Assembling and Finishing the Quilt

For detailed instructions, refer to "Quiltmaking Basics" on page 7.

1 Sew the blocks together to make a row and press the seam allowances in one direction. The quilt top should measure 24½" x 8½".

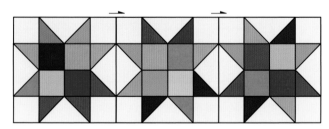

Quilt assembly

2 Layer the quilt top, batting, and backing; baste the layers together. Quilt as desired.

3 Referring to "Framing Quilts" on page 8, use the 2"-wide strips to frame your quilt. Or, referring to "Binding" on page 9, use the 2½"-wide binding strips to bind your quilt.

Autumn's Glow

Precut 5" squares in autumn's palette of gold, brown,
and rose set the tone for this star to take center stage.

Designed and pieced by Gerri Robinson.
Machine quilted by Rebecca Segura.

FINISHED QUILT: 20" x 20"
FINISHED BLOCK: 20" x 20"

Materials

Yardage is based on 42"-wide fabric unless otherwise noted.

38 squares, 5" x 5", of assorted dark and medium prints
⅝ yard of cream solid for background
¼ yard of fabric for framing or binding
1 yard of fabric for backing
30" x 30" piece of batting

Cutting

From the assorted 5" squares, cut *a total of:*

4 squares, 4½" x 4½"
4 rectangles, 2½" x 4½"
28 squares, 2⅞" x 2⅞"
16 squares, 2½" x 2½"

From the cream solid, cut:

4 rectangles, 2½" x 4½"
28 squares, 2⅞" x 2⅞"
28 squares, 2½" x 2½"

From the framing or binding fabric, cut:*

3 border strips, 2" x 42"

**For binding, cut 3 strips, 2½" x 42"*

Making the Units

1 Sew a cream 2⅞" square to each assorted 2⅞" square to make half-square-triangle units. The units should measure 2½" square. Make a total of 56 units.

Make 56

2 Use two assorted 2½" squares and one cream 2½" x 4½" rectangle to make a flying-geese unit.

The unit should measure 2½" x 4½". Make a total of four cream units.

Make 4.

3 Use two cream 2½" squares and one assorted 2½" x 4½" rectangle to make a flying-geese unit. The unit should measure 2½" x 4½". Make a total of four assorted-print units.

Make 4.

4 Sew four cream 2½" squares to one print 4½" square to make a square-in-a-square unit. The unit should measure 4½" square. Make a total of four units.

Make 4.

5 Sew four 2½" assorted squares together to make a four-patch unit. Press the seam allowances in the directions indicated. The unit should measure 4½" square.

Make 1.

Assembling the Quilt Top

1 Lay out one print 2½" square, one cream 2½" square, and 14 half-square-triangle units in four rows, making sure to orient the units as shown. Sew the pieces together into rows. Press the seam allowances in opposite directions from row to row. Sew the rows together and press the seam allowances in one direction. The pieced section should measure 8½" x 8½". Make a total of four sections.

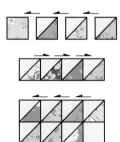 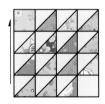

Make 4.

2 Lay out one cream flying-geese unit, one print flying-geese unit, and one square-in-a-square unit as shown. Sew the units together to make a pieced strip. Press the seam allowances away from the center. The pieced strip should measure 4½" x 8½". Make four.

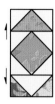

Make 4.

3 Sew pieced sections from step 1 to opposite sides of a pieced strip from step 2 as shown to make a row. Press the seam allowances away from the center. The row should measure 8½" x 20½". Make two rows.

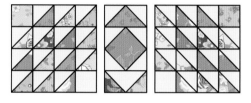

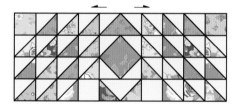

Make 2.

4 Sew pieced strips from step 2 to opposite sides of the four-patch unit as shown to make the center row. Press the seam allowances toward the center. The row should measure 4½" x 20½".

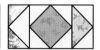

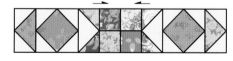

Make 1.

5 Lay out the three rows as shown. Sew the rows together to complete the quilt top. Press the seam allowances toward the center. The quilt top should measure 20½" square.

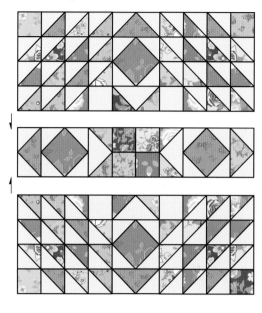

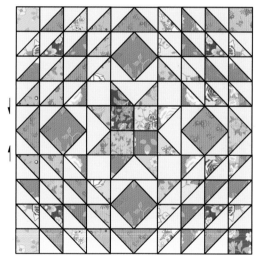

Quilt assembly

Finishing the Quilt

For detailed instructions, refer to "Quiltmaking Basics" on page 7.

1 Layer the quilt top, batting, and backing; baste the layers together. Quilt as desired.

2 Referring to "Framing Quilts" on page 8, use the 2"-wide strips to frame your quilt. Or, referring to "Binding" on page 9, use the 2½"-wide binding strips to bind your quilt.

Wild Rose Mini Sampler

Wild roses are sprinkled among twinkling stars and tumbling blocks in a simple but dramatic mini sampler.

FINISHED QUILT: 24" x 24"
FINISHED BLOCK: 8" x 8"

Materials

Yardage is based on 42"-wide fabric unless otherwise noted.

24 squares, 5" x 5", of assorted dark and medium prints for blocks and border
8 squares, 5" x 5", of assorted light prints for blocks
⅜ yard of cream solid for block background and border
1 piece, at least 5" x 8" *each,* of assorted dark-rose, medium-green, light-green, and gold wool for appliqués
1 piece, at least 7" x 12", of medium-rose wool for appliqué
¼ yard of fabric for framing *OR* binding
1 yard of fabric for backing
30" x 30" piece of batting
Fabric glue

Cutting

Appliqué patterns are on page 21.

From *each* of 8 assorted light squares, cut:
1 square, 4½" x 4½" (8 total)

From the assorted dark and medium squares, cut a total of:
20 rectangles, 2½" x 4½"
56 squares, 2½" x 2½"

From the cream solid, cut:
2 rectangles, 4½" x 12½"
2 rectangles, 4½" x 8½"
8 rectangles, 2½" x 4½"
8 squares, 2½" x 2½"

From the dark-rose wool, cut:
2 large flowers

From the medium-rose wool, cut:
4 large flowers
4 small flowers

From the medium-green wool, cut:
4 large leaves

From the light-green wool, cut:
8 small leaves

From the gold wool, cut:
6 large circles
4 small circles

From the framing or binding fabric, cut:*
2 border strips, 2" x 42"

For binding, cut 2 strips, 2½" x 42"

Making the Star Blocks

1 Sew four dark or medium 2½" squares together to make a four-patch unit. Press the seam allowances in the directions indicated. The unit should measure 4½" square. Make two units.

Make 2.

2 Use two dark or medium 2½" squares and one cream 2½" x 4½" rectangle to make a flying-geese unit. The unit should measure 2½" x 4½". Make a total of eight units.

Make 8.

3 Sew two flying-geese units from step 2 to opposite sides of a four-patch unit as shown to make a center unit. Press the seam allowances toward the center. The unit should measure 4½" x 8½". Make two units.

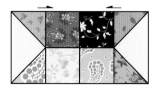

Make 2.

4 Sew a cream 2½" square to each end of the remaining flying-geese units to make 2½" x 8½" strips. Press the seam allowances toward the cream squares. Make a total of four strips.

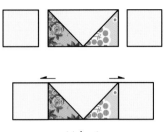

Make 4.

5 Sew two pieced strips from step 4 and one center unit from step 3 together to complete a Star block. Press the seam allowances toward the center. The block should measure 8½" square. Make a total of two blocks.

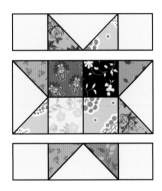

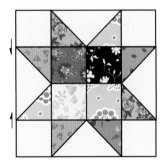

Make 2.

Making the Square-in-a-Square Blocks

1 Sew four print 2½" squares to one light 4½" square to make a square-in-a-square unit. Make eight units.

Make 8.

2 Lay out four units in a four-patch arrangement as shown. Sew the units into rows. Press the seam allowances in opposite directions from row to row. Join the rows to complete a Square-in-a-Square block. Press the seam allowances in one direction. The block should measure 8½" square. Make a total of two blocks.

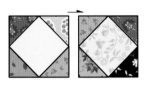

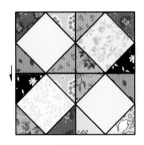

Make 2.

Assembling the Quilt Top

1 Lay out the blocks in two rows of two blocks each as shown. Sew the blocks together into rows. Press the seam allowances in opposite directions from row to row. Join the rows to complete the quilt center. Press the seam allowances in one direction. The quilt center should measure 16½" x 16½".

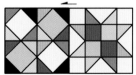

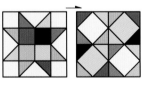

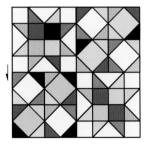

2 Sew four assorted 2½" x 4½" rectangles together along their long edges. Press the seam allowances in one direction. Make two strips. Sew a pieced strip to one end of a cream 4½" x 8½" rectangle to make a side border strip. Press the seam allowances toward the pieced strip. The border strip should measure 4½" x 16½". Make two.

Make 2. Make 2.

3 Sew six assorted 2½" x 4½" rectangles together along their long edges. Press the seam allowances in one direction. Make two strips. Sew a pieced strip to one end of a cream 4½" x 12½" rectangle to make a top border strip. Press the seam allowances toward the pieced strip. The border strip should measure 4½" x 24½". Repeat to make a bottom border strip.

Make 2. Make 2.

4 Sew the border strips from step 2 to opposite sides of the quilt center. Press the seam allowances toward the border strips. Then sew the border strips

from step 3 to the top and bottom of the quilt. The quilt top should measure 24½" x 24½".

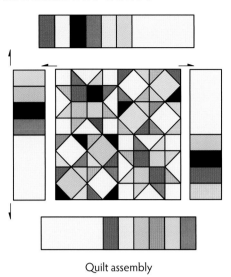

Quilt assembly

Wool Appliqué

Prepare the wool appliqués as described in "Wool Appliqué" on page 8. Position and baste the flowers, circles, and leaves on the outer border.

Finishing the Quilt

For detailed instructions, refer to "Quiltmaking Basics" on page 7.

1 Layer the quilt top, batting, and backing; baste the layers together. Quilt as desired.

2 Referring to "Framing Quilts" on page 8, use the 2"-wide strips to frame your quilt. Or, referring to "Binding" on page 9, use the 2½"-wide binding strips to bind your quilt.

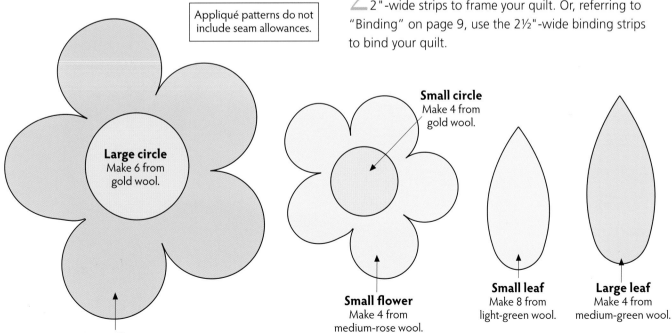

Appliqué patterns do not include seam allowances.

Large circle
Make 6 from gold wool.

Large flower
Make 2 from dark-rose wool and 4 from medium-rose wool.

Small circle
Make 4 from gold wool.

Small flower
Make 4 from medium-rose wool.

Small leaf
Make 8 from light-green wool.

Large leaf
Make 4 from medium-green wool.

Gelato

Scoop up an assortment of precut 5" squares in a rainbow of colors and you're on your way to whetting your appetite for a fun and refreshing treat.

Materials

Yardage is based on 42"-wide fabric unless otherwise noted.

40 squares, 5" x 5", of assorted bright prints for blocks
2 yards of white solid for block background, pieced sashing, and inner border
1⅝ yards of floral for outer border
⅞ yard of green solid for blocks
1 fat eighth (9" x 21") *each* of blue, pink, red, and yellow solids for pieced sashing
½ yard of cream-and-green diagonal stripe for binding
3¾ yards of fabric for backing
62" x 72" piece of batting

Cutting

From the assorted bright squares, cut *a total of*:
80 rectangles, 2½" x 4½"

From the white solid, cut:
31 rectangles, 2½" x 8½"
40 squares, 2⅞" x 2⅞"
160 squares, 2½" x 2½"
4 strips, 1½" x 42"

From the green solid, cut:
40 squares, 2⅞" x 2⅞"
80 squares, 2½" x 2½"

From *each* of the blue, pink, red, and yellow solids, cut:
3 squares, 2½" x 2½" (12 total)
24 squares, 1½" x 1½" (96 total)

From the *lengthwise grain* of the floral, cut:
2 strips, 6½" x 54"
2 strips, 6½" x 56"

From the cream-and-green diagonal stripe, cut:
7 strips, 2½" x 42"

TECHNIQUES USED

- Half-Square-Triangle Units (page 7)
- Flying-Geese Units (page 7)
- Pieced Sashing (page 8)

Designed and pieced by Gerri Robinson.
Machine quilted by Rebecca Segura.

FINISHED QUILT: 52" x 62½"
FINISHED BLOCK: 8" x 8"

Making the Blocks

1 Sew a white 2⅞" square to each green 2⅞" square to make half-square-triangle units. The units should measure 2½" square. Make a total of 80 units.

Make 80.

2 Sew a green 2½" square and a white 2½" square to each bright print 2½" x 4½" rectangle to make a flying-geese unit. The unit should measure 2½" x 4½". Make a total of 80 units.

Make 80.

3 Sew a white 2½" square to a half-square-triangle unit as shown. Press the seam allowances toward the green triangle. Sew the pieced unit to the top of

a flying-geese unit to make a quadrant. Press the seam allowances in the directions indicated. Make 80 quadrants.

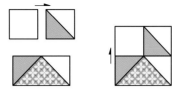

Make 80.

4 Sew four quadrants together to make a block. Press the seam allowances in the directions indicated. The block should measure 8½" square. Make a total of 20 blocks.

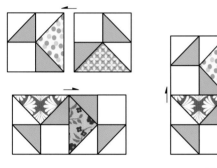

Make 20.

Making the Pieced Sashing

1 Sew two blue 1½" squares to one end of a white 2½" x 8½" rectangle to make a single pieced-sashing unit. Make a total of five blue, four pink, three red, and two yellow units.

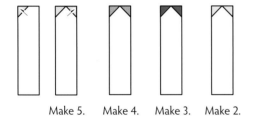

Make 5.   Make 4.   Make 3.   Make 2.

2 Sew two blue 1½" squares and two pink 1½" squares to the ends of a white 2½" x 8½" rectangle as shown to make a double pieced-sashing unit. Make two blue/pink units. Repeat to make three blue/red units, two blue/yellow units, two pink/red units, four pink/yellow units, and four yellow/red units.

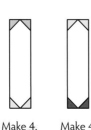

Make 2.   Make 3.   Make 2.   Make 2.   Make 4.   Make 4.

Assembling the Quilt Top

1 Lay out the blocks; pieced-sashing units; and blue, pink, red, and yellow 2½" squares as shown in the quilt assembly diagram below, making sure to orient the pieced-sashing units as shown. The triangle corners should make small stars when the strips are positioned correctly. Once you're satisfied with the arrangement, sew the pieces together into rows. Press the seam allowances toward the pieced-sashing units.

2 Join the rows and press the seam allowances toward the sashing rows. The quilt top should measure 38½" x 48½".

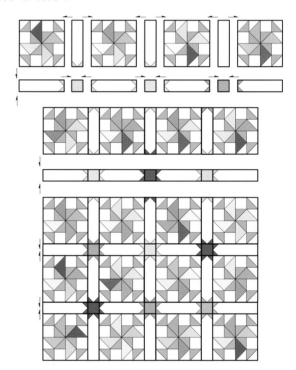

Quilt assembly

3 Join the 1½"-wide white strips end to end to make a long strip. Referring to "Adding Borders" on page 9, measure and cut the inner-border strips; then sew them to the quilt top. Press the seam allowances toward the inner border.

4 Repeat to add the floral outer-border strips to the quilt top. Press the seam allowances toward the outer border.

Finishing the Quilt

For detailed instructions, refer to "Quiltmaking Basics" on page 7.

1 Layer the quilt top, batting, and backing; baste the layers together. Quilt as desired.

2 Referring to "Binding" on page 9, use the cream-and-green 2½"-wide strips to bind your quilt.

Squares of Delight

Delight in the wonder of the creations that stem
from a mere 10" square of fabric.

Galaxy

A single block with simple construction, when merged together with others just like it, creates a galaxy of stars.

Materials

Yardage is based on 42"-wide fabric unless otherwise noted.

36 squares, 10" x 10", of assorted cream and tan prints for blocks

27 squares, 10" x 10", of assorted blue, brown, and black prints for blocks

1⅝ yards of blue stripe for outer border

⅝ yard of dark-blue print for binding

4 yards of fabric for backing

70" x 70" piece of batting

Cutting

From the assorted cream and tan squares, cut a total of:

36 squares, 4½" x 4½"

432 squares, 2½" x 2½"

From the assorted blue, brown, and black squares, cut a total of:

144 rectangles, 2½" x 4½"

144 squares, 2½" x 2½"

From the blue stripe, cut:

8 strips, 6½" x 42"

From the dark-blue print, cut:

7 strips, 2½" x 42"

TECHNIQUES USED

- Flying-Geese Units (page 7)
- Square-in-a-Square Units (page 7)

Making the Blocks

1 Sew four blue, brown, or black 2½" squares to one cream or tan 4½" square to make a square-in-a-square unit. The unit should measure 4½" square. Make a total of 36 units.

Make 36.

2 Sew two cream or tan 2½" squares to one blue, brown, or black 2½" x 4½" rectangle to make a

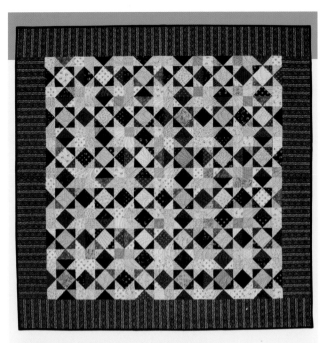

Designed and pieced by Gerri Robinson. Machine quilted by Rebecca Segura.

FINISHED QUILT: 60½" x 60½"
FINISHED BLOCK: 8" x 8"

flying-geese unit. The unit should measure 2½" x 4½". Make a total of 144 units.

Make 144.

3 Sew two flying-geese units from step 2 to opposite sides of a square-in-a-square unit from step 1 as shown to make a center unit. Press the seam allowances toward the center. The unit should measure 4½" x 8½". Make a total of 36 units.

Make 36.

4 Sew a cream or tan 2½" square to each end of the remaining flying-geese units to make 2½" x 8½" strips. Press the seam allowances toward the cream squares. Make a total of 72 strips.

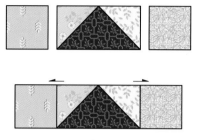

Make 72.

5 Sew two pieced strips from step 4 and one center unit from step 3 together to complete a Star block. Press the seam allowances away from the center. The block should measure 8½" square. Make a total of 36 blocks.

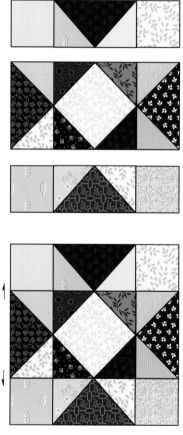

Make 36.

Assembling the Quilt Top

1 Lay out the blocks in six rows of six blocks each as shown. Sew the blocks together into rows. Press the seam allowances in opposite directions from row to row. Join the rows and press the seam allowances in one direction. The quilt top should measure 48½" square.

Quilt assembly

2 Join two blue striped strips to make a pieced strip. Make a total of four pieced strips. Referring to "Adding Borders" on page 9, measure and cut the border strips, and then sew them to the quilt top. Press the seam allowances toward the outer border.

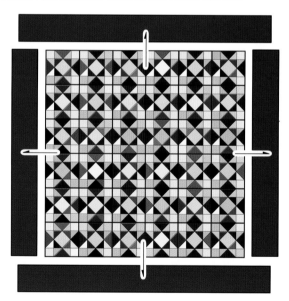

Finishing the Quilt

For detailed instructions, refer to "Quiltmaking Basics" on page 7.

1 Layer the quilt top, batting, and backing; baste the layers together. Quilt as desired.

2 Referring to "Binding" on page 9, use the dark-blue 2½"-wide strips to bind your quilt.

Friendship

The intertwined pinwheels remind me of the "pinky promise" I made with my best friend, promising to keep her secrets near and dear to my heart.

Materials

Yardage is based on 42"-wide fabric unless otherwise noted.

36 squares, 10" x 10", of assorted dark and medium prints for blocks

2⅝ yard of cream solid for block background

1⅞ yards of red print for outer border and binding

4 yards of fabric for backing

70" x 70" piece of batting

Cutting

From *each* of the assorted dark and medium squares, cut:*

4 rectangles, 2½" x 4½" (144 total)

2 squares, 2⅞" x 2⅞" (72 total)

*If desired, set aside the leftover fabrics to use for "Do-Si-Do" on page 32.

From the cream solid, cut:

72 squares, 2⅞" x 2⅞"

432 squares, 2½" x 2½"

From the *lengthwise grain* of the red print, cut:

2 strips, 6½" x 64"

2 strips, 6½" x 52"

5 strips, 2½" x 52"

TECHNIQUES USED

- Half-Square-Triangle Units (page 7)
- Flying-Geese Units (page 7)

Making the Blocks

1 Sew a cream 2⅞" square to each assorted 2⅞" square to make half-square-triangle units. The units should measure 2½" square. Make a total of 36 sets of four matching units (144 total).

Make 144.

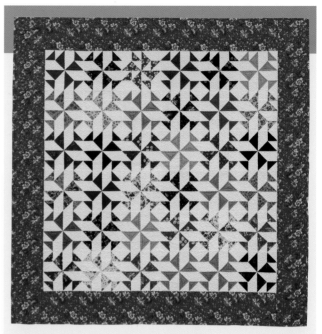

Designed and pieced by Gerri Robinson.
Machine quilted by Rebecca Segura.

FINISHED QUILT: 60½" x 60½"
FINISHED BLOCK: 8" x 8"

2 Sew two cream 2½" squares to one medium or dark 2½" x 4½" rectangle to make a flying-geese unit. The unit should measure 2½" x 4½". Make a total of 36 sets of four matching flying-geese units (144 total).

Make 144.

3 Sew a cream 2½" square and a half-square-triangle unit together as shown. Press the seam allowances toward the triangle. Sew the pieced unit to the top of a matching flying-geese unit to make a quadrant. Press the seam allowances in the direction indicated. The quadrant should measure 4½" square. Make a total of 36 sets of four matching quadrants (144 total).

Make 144.

4 Sew four matching quadrants together to make a block. Press the seam allowances in the directions indicated. The block should measure 8½" square. Make a total of 36 blocks.

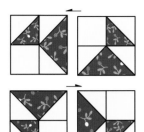

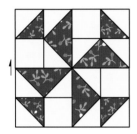

Make 36.

Assembling the Quilt Top

1 Lay out the blocks in six rows of six blocks each as shown. Sew the blocks together into rows. Press the seam allowances in opposite directions from row to row. Join the rows and press the seam allowances in one direction. The quilt top should measure 48½" square.

Quilt assembly

2 Referring to "Adding Borders" on page 9, measure and trim the red 6½"-wide outer-border strips and sew them to the quilt top. Press the seam allowances toward the outer border.

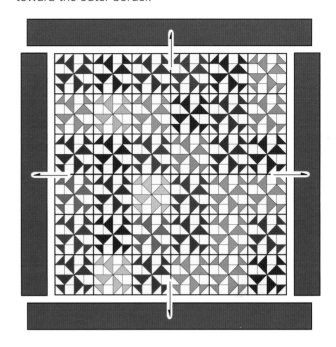

Finishing the Quilt

For detailed instructions, refer to "Quiltmaking Basics" on page 7.

1 Layer the quilt top, batting, and backing; baste the layers together. Quilt as desired.

2 Referring to "Binding" on page 9, use the red 2½"-wide strips to bind your quilt.

Do-Si-Do

Elongated pinwheels do-si-do around a center star. Use leftovers from "Friendship" on page 29, or start with a fresh batch of fabrics.

Materials

Yardage is based on 42"-wide fabric unless otherwise noted.

33 rectangles, 2½" x 10", of assorted dark and medium prints for blocks*

4 squares, 3" x 3", of assorted dark and medium prints for blocks*

1⅓ yards of cream solid for block background

⅜ yard of fabric for framing or binding

1⅓ yards of fabric for backing

42" x 42" piece of batting

If desired, you can use leftovers from "Friendship" on page 29.

Cutting

From the assorted dark and medium rectangles, cut *a total of*:

64 rectangles, 2½" x 4½"

4 squares, 2½" x 2½"

From the assorted dark and medium squares, cut *a total of*:

4 squares, 2⅞" x 2⅞"

From the cream solid, cut:

12 squares, 4½" x 4½"

32 rectangles, 2½" x 4½"

4 squares, 2⅞" x 2⅞"

132 squares, 2½" x 2½"

From the framing or binding fabric, cut:*

4 border strips, 2" x 42"

For binding, cut 4 strips, 2½" x 42"

TECHNIQUES USED

- Half-Square-Triangle Units (page 7)
- Quick-Angled Rectangles (page 7)

Making the Blocks

1 Sew a cream 2⅞" square to each assorted 2⅞" square to make half-square-triangle units. The units should measure 2½" square. Make eight units.

Make 8.

2 Sew a cream 2½" square to each end of the assorted 2½" x 4½" rectangles as shown to make

Designed and pieced by Gerri Robinson.
Machine quilted by Rebecca Segura.

FINISHED QUILT: 32" x 32"
FINISHED BLOCK: 16" x 16"

rectangular units. The units should measure 2½" x 4½". Make 64 units.

Make 64.

3 Sew two rectangular units from step 2 together to make a 4½" square. Press the seam allowances in one direction. Make 16 units.

Make 16.

4 Sew a cream 2½" x 4½" rectangle to the left side of a rectangular unit from step 2 to make a 4½" square. Press the seam allowances toward the cream rectangle. Make 32 units.

Make 32.

5 Lay out one cream 2½" square, two half-square-triangle units, and one dark or medium 2½" square in a four-patch arrangement as shown. Join the pieces into rows. Press the seam allowances toward the squares. Then join the rows to make a corner unit and press the seam allowances in one direction. Make a total of four corner units.

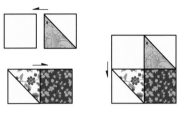

Make 4.

6 Lay out three cream 4½" squares, eight units from step 4, four units from step 3, and one unit from step 5 in four rows as shown. Join the pieces into rows. Press the seam allowances in opposite directions from row to row. Join the rows to complete the block; press the seam allowances in one direction. Make four blocks.

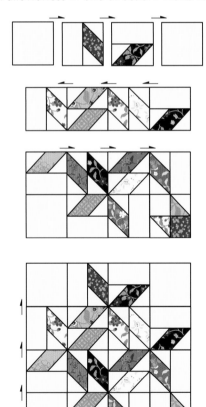

Make 4.

Assembling and Finishing the Quilt

For detailed instructions, refer to "Quiltmaking Basics" on page 7.

1 Lay out the blocks in two rows of two blocks each, rotating the blocks to form a star in the center of the block. Sew the blocks together in rows. Press the seam allowances in the directions indicated. Then sew the rows together and press the seam allowances in one direction. The quilt top should measure 32½" square.

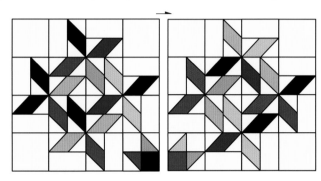

Quilt assembly

2 Layer the quilt top, batting, and backing; baste the layers together. Quilt as desired.

3 Referring to "Framing Quilts" on page 8, use the 2"-wide strips to frame you quilt. Or, referring to "Binding" on page 9, use the 2½"-wide binding strips to bind your quilt.

Dancing among the Stars

*Pinwheels twist and twirl in a highly choreographed
fashion amongst the brightly colored stars.*

Designed and pieced by Gerri Robinson.
Machine quilted by Rebecca Segura.

FINISHED QUILT: 90½" x 90½"   **FINISHED STAR BLOCK:** 8" x 8"
FINISHED PINWHEEL BLOCK: 4" x 4"

Materials

Yardage is based on 42"-wide fabric unless otherwise noted.

5¼ yards of cream solid for block background and
    inner border
2¾ yards of blue floral for outer border
½ yard *each* of 5 assorted bright solids for
    Star blocks
36 squares, 10" x 10", of assorted bright prints for
    Pinwheel blocks
⅞ yard of diagonal plaid for binding
8¾ yards of fabric for backing
100" x 100" piece of batting

TECHNIQUES USED

- Half-Square-Triangle Units (page 7)
- Quick-Angled Rectangles (page 7)

Cutting

From *each* square of assorted bright prints, cut:
8 squares, 2⅞" x 2⅞" (288 total)

From the cream solid, cut:
20 rectangles, 4½" x 8½"
40 squares, 4½" x 4½"
100 rectangles, 2½" x 4½"
288 squares, 2⅞" x 2⅞"
100 squares, 2½" x 2½"
8 strips, 1½" x 42"

From *each* of the 5 assorted bright solids, cut:
5 squares, 4½" x 4½" (25 total)
40 squares, 2½" x 2½" (200 total)

From the *lengthwise grain* of the blue floral, cut:
2 strips, 8½" x 94"
2 strips, 8½" x 78"

From the diagonal plaid, cut:
10 strips, 2½" x 42"

Making the Pinwheel Blocks

1 Sew a cream 2⅞" square to each bright-print 2⅞" square to make half-square-triangle units. The units should measure 2½" square. Make a total of 576 units.

Make 576.

2 Sew four half-square-triangle units together as shown to make a Pinwheel block. Press the seam allowances in the directions indicated. The block should measure 4½" square. Make a total of 144 blocks.

Make 144.

3 Sew two Pinwheel blocks together and press the seam allowances in one direction. The two-block unit should measure 4½" x 8½". Make a total of 60 units. Set aside the remaining 24 Pinwheel blocks.

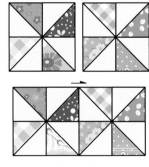

Make 60.

Making the Star Blocks

1 Use two matching bright-solid 2½" squares and one cream 2½" x 4½" rectangle to make a flying-geese unit. The unit should measure 2½" x 4½". Make a total of 20 sets of four matching flying-geese units of *each* color (100 total).

Make 100.

2 Sew two matching flying-geese units to opposite sides of a matching bright-solid 4½" square as shown to make a center unit. Press the seam allowances toward the center. The unit should measure 4½" x 8½". Make a total of five units of *each* color (25 total).

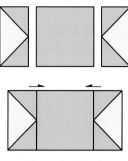

Make 5 of each color
(25 total).

3 Sew a cream 2½" square to each end of the remaining flying-geese units to make 2½" x 8½" strips. Press the seam allowances toward the cream squares. Make a total of 10 units of *each* color (50 total).

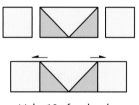

Make 10 of each color
(50 total).

4 Sew two matching pieced strips from step 4 and one matching center unit from step 3 together to complete a Star block. Press the seam allowances toward the center. The block should measure 8½" square. Make a total of 25 blocks.

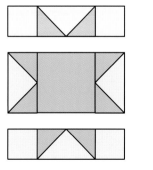 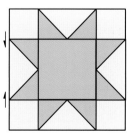

Make 25.

Assembling the Quilt Top

1 Lay out six Pinwheel blocks, five cream 4½" x 8½" rectangles, and two cream 4½" squares as shown. Sew the pieces together to make the top row. Press the seam allowances toward the cream squares and rectangles. The row should measure 4½" x 72½". Repeat to make the bottom row.

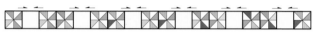

Top/bottom border
Make 2.

2 Lay out two Pinwheel blocks, six cream 4½" squares, and five two-block units as shown. Sew the pieces together to make a sashing row. Press the seam allowances toward the cream squares. The row should measure 4½" x 72½". Make six rows.

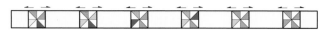

Sashing row
Make 6.

3 Lay out two cream 4½" x 8½" rectangles, six two-block units, and five Star blocks, as shown. Sew the pieces together to make a block row. Press the seam allowances toward the cream rectangles and Star blocks. The row should measure 8½" x 72½". Make five rows.

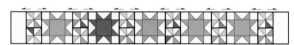

Block row
Make 5.

4 Lay out the rows as shown in the quilt assembly diagram. Join the rows and press the seam allowances toward the sashing rows. The quilt top should measure 72½" square.

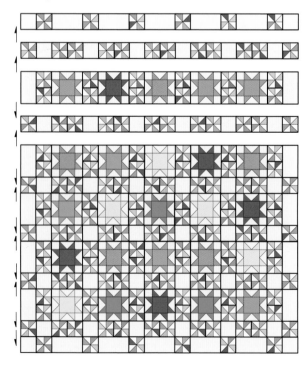

Quilt assembly

5 Join the cream 1½"-wide strips end to end to make a long strip. Referring to "Adding Borders" on page 9, measure and cut the inner-border strips, and then sew them to the quilt top. Press the seam allowances toward the inner border.

6 Repeat to add the blue-floral 8½"-wide outer-border strips to the quilt top. Press the seam allowances toward the outer border.

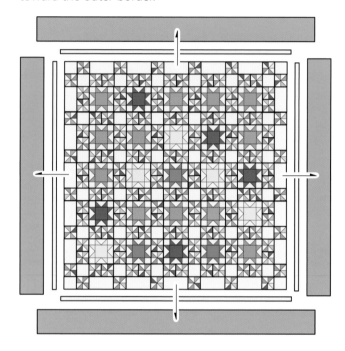

Finishing the Quilt

For detailed instructions, refer to "Quiltmaking Basics" on page 7.

1 Layer the quilt top, batting, and backing; baste the layers together. Quilt as desired.

2 Referring to "Binding" on page 9, use the plaid 2½"-wide strips to bind your quilt.

Fabric Ribbons

Strips of fabric, 2½" wide, resembling freshly unwound ribbon
from a spool, offer endless design possibilities for quilts.

Buttoned Up

The exact placement of fabric and buttons give this quilt its buttoned-up look.

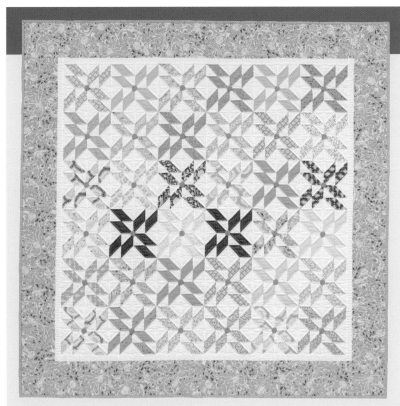

Designed and pieced by Gerri Robinson.
Machine quilted by Rebecca Segura.

FINISHED QUILT: 62½" x 62½" **FINISHED BLOCK:** 8" x 8"

Materials

Yardage is based on 42"-wide fabric unless otherwise noted.

36 strips, 2½" x 42", of assorted bright prints for blocks
3 yards of white solid for block background and inner border
2 yards of teal print for outer border
⅝ yard of orange print for binding
4¼ yards of fabric for backing
72" x 72" piece of batting
36 orange buttons, ⅞" diameter

Cutting

From *each* of the assorted bright strips, cut:
8 rectangles, 2½" x 4½" (288 total)

From the white solid, cut:
576 squares, 2½" x 2½"
5 strips, 1½" x 42"

From the *lengthwise grain* of the teal print, cut:
2 strips, 6½" x 54"
2 strips, 6½" x 66"

From the orange print, cut:
7 strips, 2½" x 42"

TECHNIQUE USED

• Quick-Angled Rectangles (page 7)

Making the Blocks

1 Sew two white 2½" squares and one bright 2½" x 4½" rectangle together as shown to make a rectangular unit. Make a total of 36 sets of eight matching units (288 total).

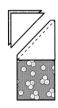

Make 288.

2 Sew two matching units from step 1 together as shown to make a 4½" square. Press the seam allowances in one direction. Make a total of 144 units.

Make 144.

3 Sew four matching units from step 2 together, rotating them as shown, to make a block. The block should measure 8½" square. Make a total of 36 blocks.

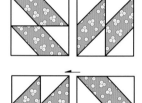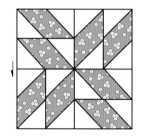

Make 36.

Assembling the Quilt Top

1 Lay out the blocks in six rows of six blocks each. Sew the blocks together in rows. Press the seam allowances in opposite directions from row to row. Sew the rows together and press the seam allowances in one direction. The quilt center should measure 48½" square.

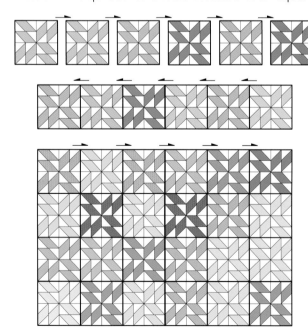

Quilt assembly

2 Join the white 1½"-wide strips end to end to make a long strip. Referring to "Adding Borders" on page 9, measure and cut the inner-border strips, and then sew them to the quilt top. Press the seam allowances toward the inner border.

3 Repeat to add the teal 6½"-wide outer-border strips. Press the seam allowances toward the outer border.

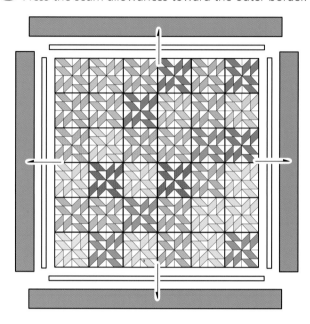

Finishing the Quilt

For detailed instructions, refer to "Quiltmaking Basics" on page 7.

1 Layer the quilt top, batting, and backing; baste the layers together. Quilt as desired.

2 Referring to "Binding" on page 9, use the orange 2½"-wide strips to bind your quilt.

3 Sew an orange button in the center of each block.

Carefree

Piecing the blocks in a random and scrappy fashion results in a carefree and spirited design.

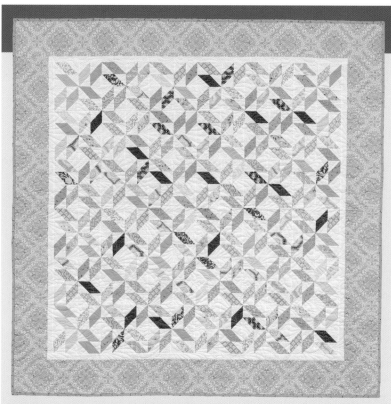

Designed and pieced by Gerri Robinson.
Machine quilted by Rebecca Segura.

FINISHED QUILT: 62½" x 62½" **FINISHED BLOCK:** 8" x 8"

Materials

Yardage is based on 42"-wide fabric unless otherwise noted.

36 strips, 2½" x 42", of assorted bright fabrics for blocks
3 yards of white solid for block background and inner border
2 yards of orange print for outer border
⅝ yard of teal print for binding
4¼ yards of fabric for backing
72" x 72" piece of batting

Cutting

From *each* of the 36 strips of bright fabric, cut:
8 rectangles, 2½" x 4½" (288 total)

From the white solid, cut:
576 squares, 2½" x 2½"
5 strips, 1½" x 42"

From the *lengthwise grain* of the orange print, cut:
2 strips, 6½" x 54"
2 strips, 6½" x 66"

From the teal print, cut:
7 strips, 2½" x 42"

TECHNIQUE USED

• Quick-Angled Rectangles (page 7)

Making the Blocks

For detailed illustrations on the following techniques refer to "Making the Blocks" on page 41.

1 Sew two white 2½" squares and one bright 2½" x 4½" rectangle together as shown to make a rectangular unit. Make a total of 288 units.

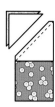

Make 288.

2 Randomly sew two units from step 1 together to make a 4½" square. Press the seam allowances in one direction. Make a total of 144 units.

3 Randomly sew four units from step 2 together to make a block. Press the seam allowances in the directions indicated. The block should measure 8½" square. Make a total of 36 blocks.

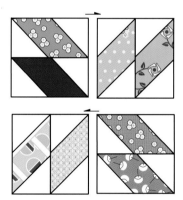

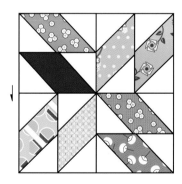

Make 36.

Assembling the Quilt Top

1 Arrange and sew the blocks together into six rows of six blocks each; press the seam allowances in opposite directions from row to row. Then sew the rows together and press the seam allowances in one direction.

2 Join the white 1½"-wide strips end to end. Measure and cut the inner-border strips; then sew them to the quilt top. Press the seam allowances toward the inner border.

3 Repeat to add the orange 6½"-wide outer-border strips. Press the seam allowances toward the outer border.

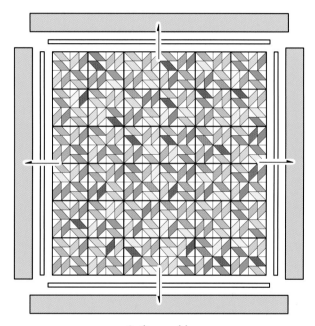

Quilt assembly

Finishing the Quilt

For detailed instructions, refer to "Quiltmaking Basics" on page 7.

1 Layer the quilt top, batting, and backing; baste the layers together. Quilt as desired.

2 Referring to "Binding" on page 9, use the teal 2½"-wide strips to bind your quilt.

Buttoned Up Boxed Cushion

Button-tufted pinwheels twist and twirl across this box-style cushion.

Materials

Yardage is based on 42"-wide fabric unless otherwise noted. Yields 1 cushion.

32 rectangles, 2½" x 4½", of bright fabrics for blocks*
⅜ yard of white solid for blocks and piping
1 fat quarter of teal fabric for pillow backing
18" x 18" square of muslin for pillow lining
18" x 18" square of batting for pillow
3¾ yards of ¼"-diameter cotton cording for piping
10 orange buttons, ⅞" diameter
16" x 16" pillow form or polyester fiberfill

You can use the leftover fabrics from "Carefree" on page 43 or "Buttoned Up" on page 40.

Cutting

From the white solid, cut:
20 squares, 2½" x 2½"
2"-wide bias strips to total 130"

From the teal fabric, cut:
1 square, 16½" x 16½"
2 strips, 4" x 32½"

> ### TECHNIQUE USED
> • Quick-Angled Rectangles (page 7)

Making the Cushion Top

1 Sew a 2½" white square to a bright rectangle as shown to make a rectangular unit. Make 20 units.

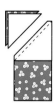

Make 20.

2 Sew one unit from step 1 and one bright rectangle together as shown to make a 4½" square. Press the seam allowances toward the rectangle. Make a total of 12 units.

Make 12.

Designed and pieced by Gerri Robinson.
Made by Patty Lanum.

FINISHED PILLOW: 16" x 16"
FINISHED LOCK: 8" x 8"

3 Join the remaining units from step 1 in pairs as shown to make four units. Press the seam allowances in one direction. The units should measure 4½" square.

Make 4.

4 Lay out three units from step 2 and one unit from step 3 as shown. Join the units into rows. Press the seam allowances in opposite directions from row to row. Join the rows to make a block. Press the seam allowances in one direction. The block should measure 8½" square. Make a total of four blocks.

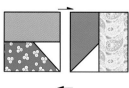 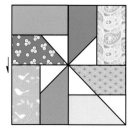

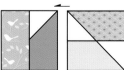

Make 4.

5 Lay out the blocks in two rows of two blocks each, rotating them as shown. Join the blocks into rows. Press the seam allowances in opposite directions from row to row. Join the rows and press the seam allowances in one direction. The cushion top should measure 16½" square.

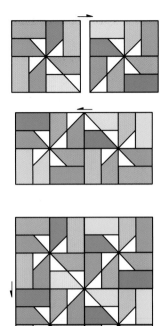

Finishing the Cushion

1 Layer the cushion top with the batting and the 18" square of muslin. Baste the layers together. Quilt as desired.

2 Trim the backing and batting even with the edges of the cushion top. Machine baste around the block about ⅛" from the outer edges.

3 Sew the white bias strips together to make a continuous strip. Use this strip to cover the cording and make the piping as described in "Covered Cording" on page 49. Trim the seam allowance evenly to ¼".

4 Align the raw edges of the cushion top and piping. Sew the piping around the edge of the cushion top with a ¼" seam allowance. Start in the middle of the bottom edge and stitch around the cushion, overlapping the beginning and ending tails of the piping as shown.

Stitch across the piping where the tails cross. Trim the ends of the piping even with the raw edge of the cushion top.

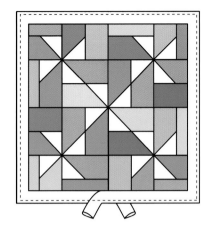

Align raw edges of piping and cushion top.
Stich ¼" from edges.

5 Repeat step 4 to sew the piping around the edge of the teal square to make the cushion bottom.

6 Join the short ends of the teal 4"-wide strips to make a continuous loop for the boxing strip. Fold the strip into quarters and lightly press to mark the corner placement, making sure the seam lines are *not* in a corner.

7 Arrange the boxing strip on the cushion top, right sides together with the raw edged aligned; place a creased lined in each corner. Sew the strip to the cushion top, stitching all around the square and stopping where you started with a backstitch. When you reach a corner, stop in the exact corner with the needle in the down position. Clip the strip almost to the needle to spread the strip around the corner. Pivot the cushion top and continue sewing, clipping each corner as you come to it.

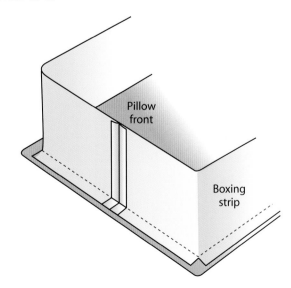

Pillow front

Boxing strip

8 Sew the boxing strip to the cushion bottom in the same way, stopping with a backstitch about 6" from where you started. Turn the cushion right side out.

9 Insert the pillow form or firmly stuff the cushion with polyester fiberfill. Turn under the ¼" seam allowance along the opening and stitch the opening closed.

10 Referring to the photo on page 47 for placement guidance, mark the position of the buttons on the cushion bottom. Thread a needle with about a 24" length of thread and knot both ends. On one of the marks, insert the needle into the cushion bottom and bring it up to the cushion top, pulling the thread through to the knot. Insert the needle through a button hole and down again through the second hole. Insert the needle back through the cushion to the back and add a button to the cushion bottom. Pull the thread very tight to create the tuft in the cushion. Continue sewing, making several more stitches to firmly attach the button to the cushion. Knot the thread on the back and clip the thread.

11 Repeat step 10 to add the remaining buttons as shown in the photo on page 47.

COVERED CORDING

Covered cording creates a line of trim along the edges of your pillow. To make covered cording follow these steps.

1 Cut bias strips the width specified in the project. Sew the strips together end to end, and press the seam allowances open.

2 To cover the cording, fold the fabric strip in half lengthwise, wrong sides together. Insert the cording, pushing it snugly against the fold.

3 Use a zipper foot on your sewing machine and set the needle so that it sews to the left of the foot. Sew the two cut edges of the fabric together, enclosing the cording.

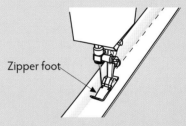

Zipper foot

4 When you've enclosed the entire piece of cording, trim the seam allowances evenly to ¼".

Buttoned Up Pillow

Remnants from "Buttoned Up" on page 40 sew up quickly
to make this companion pillow.

Materials

Yardage is based on 42"-wide fabric unless otherwise noted. Yields 1 pillow.

14 rectangles, 2½" x 4½", of bright fabrics for block*
2 squares, 4½" x 4½", of bright fabrics for block*
1 fat quarter (18" x 21") of white solid for block and piping
1 fat quarter of fabric for pillow backing
14" x 14" square of muslin for pillow lining
14" x 14" square of batting for pillow
1½ yards of ⅛"-diameter cotton cording for piping
2 orange buttons, ⅞" diameter
12" x 12" pillow form

You can use the leftover fabrics from "Carefree" on page 43 or "Buttoned Up" on page 40.

Cutting

From the white solid, cut:
8 squares, 2½" x 2½"
2"-wide bias strips to total 54"

From the pillow backing fabric, cut:
2 rectangles, 8½" x 12½"

> **TECHNIQUE USED**
> • Quick-Angled Rectangles (page 7)

Making the Pillow Top

1 Sew one white square and one bright rectangle together as shown to make a rectangular unit. Make eight units.

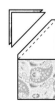

Make 8.

Designed and pieced by Gerri Robinson.
Made by Patty Lanum.

FINISHED PILLOW: 12" x 12"

2 Sew one unit from step 1 and one bright rectangle together as shown to make a 4½" square. Press the seam allowances toward the rectangle. Make a total of six units.

Make 6.

3 Join the remaining two units from step 1 as shown to make a 4½" square. Press the seam allowances in one direction.

Make 1.

4 Lay out the two bright 4½" squares and the units from steps 2 and 3 in a nine-patch arrangement as shown. Join the pieces into rows. Press the seam allowances in opposite directions from row to row. Sew the rows together and press the seam allowances away from the center.

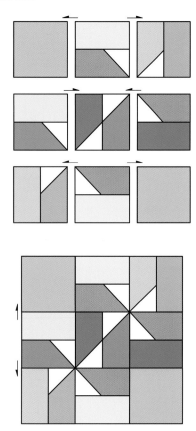

Finishing the Pillow

1 Layer the pillow top with the batting and the 14" square of muslin. Baste the layers together. Quilt as desired.

2 Trim the backing and batting even with the edges of the pillow top. Machine baste around the block about ⅛" from the outer edges.

3 Sew the white bias strips together to make a continuous strip. Use this strip to cover the cording and make the piping as described in "Covered Cording" on page 49. Trim the seam allowances evenly to ¼".

4 Align the raw edges of the pillow top and piping. Sew the piping around the edge of the pillow top with a ¼" seam allowance. Start in the middle of the bottom edge and stitch around the pillow, overlapping the beginning and ending tails of the piping as shown on page 48. Stitch across the piping where the tails cross. Trim the ends of the piping even with the raw edge of the pillow top.

5 To make the pillow back, fold over ½" on one 12½" edge of both backing rectangles, and then fold over ½" again. Press and machine stitch along the folded edge.

6 Overlap the hemmed edges approximately 4" to create a 12½" square. Machine baste along each side as shown, about ⅛" from the outer edges.

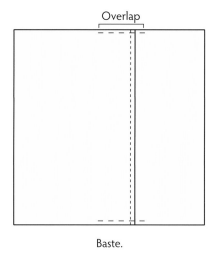

Overlap

Baste.

7 Place the pillow front on top of the back of the pillow, right sides together. With the pillow top on top, sew around the edges with a ¼" seam allowance. Clip the corners and turn the pillow right sides out.

8 Add buttons as desired. Insert the pillow form through the opening.

Double Delights

Double your pleasure while creating with 9"x 21" strips of fabric. The delight is yours when a simple fabric strip creates two equally charming and delightful designs.

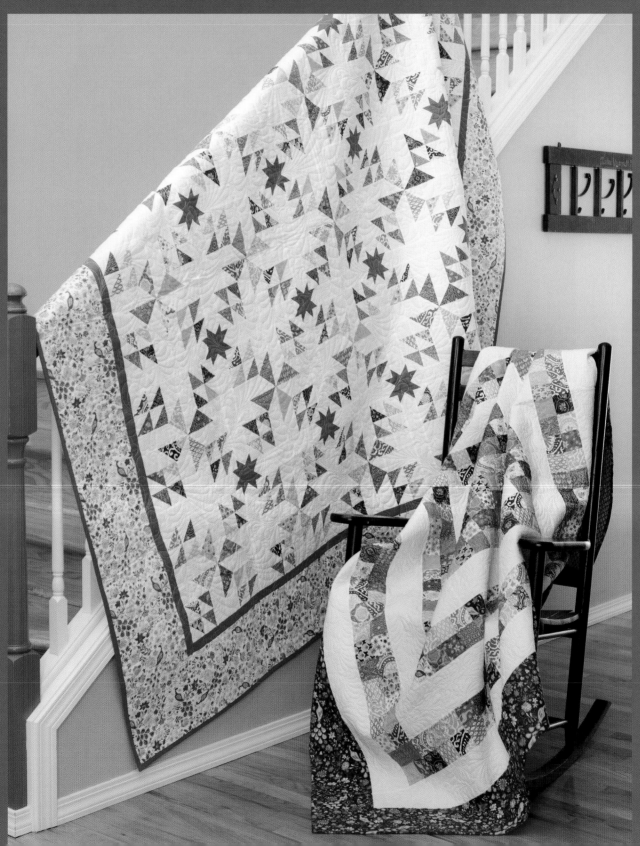

Summer Time

The sights and sounds of summer are captured in this bright and cheerful quilt.

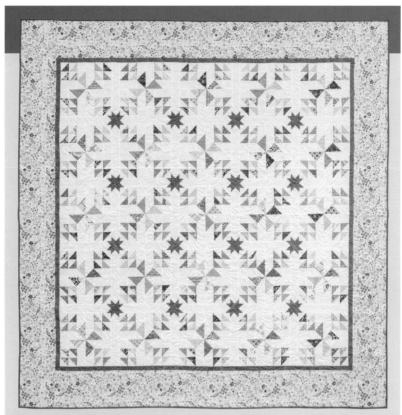

Designed and pieced by Gerri Robinson.
Machine quilted by Rebecca Segura.

FINISHED QUILT: 86½" x 86½"   **FINISHED BLOCK:** 12" x 12"

Materials

Yardage is based on 42"-wide fabric unless otherwise noted.

5 yards of white solid for block background and sashing
1 fat eighth (9" x 21") *each* of 40 assorted bright prints for blocks
2½ yards of multicolored print for outer border
1⅓ yards of raspberry solid for sashing stars, inner border, and binding
8⅜ yards of fabric for backing
96" x 96" piece of batting

Cutting

From the assorted bright prints, cut *a total of:**
100 rectangles, 2½" x 4½"
200 squares, 2⅞" x 2⅞"

*If desired, set aside the leftover fabrics to use for "A 'Digital' Trip around the World" on page 58.

From the white solid, cut:
40 rectangles, 2½" x 12½"
100 rectangles, 2½" x 4½"
200 squares, 2⅞" x 2⅞"
300 squares, 2½" x 2½"

From the raspberry solid, cut:
16 squares, 2½" x 2½"
128 squares, 1½" x 1½"
7 strips, 1½" x 42"
9 strips, 2½" x 42"

From the *lengthwise grain* of the multicolored print, cut:
2 strips, 8½" x 76"
2 strips, 8½" x 90"

TECHNIQUES USED

- Half-Square-Triangle Units (page 7)
- Flying-Geese Units (page 7)
- Pieced Sashing (page 8)

Making the Blocks

1 Sew a white 2⅞" square to each bright 2⅞" square to make half-square-triangle units. The units should measure 2½" square. Make a total of 400 units.

Make 400.

2 Lay out four half-square-triangle units from step 1 as shown. Sew the units together to make a 4½" square. Press the seam allowances in the directions indicated. Make 100 units.

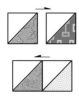

Make 100.

3 Sew a white 2½" x 4½" rectangle to the bottom of each unit. Press the seam allowances toward the rectangle. The unit should measure 4½" x 6½". Make 100 units.

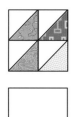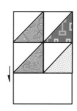

Make 100.

4 Use two white 2½" squares and one bright 2½" x 4½" rectangle to make a flying-geese unit. The unit should measure 2½" x 4½". Make a total of 100 units.

Make 100.

5 Sew a white 2½" square to one end of each flying-geese unit as shown. Press the seam allowances toward the square. The pieced unit should measure 2½" x 6½". Make 100 units.

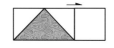

Make 100.

6 Sew a unit from step 3 to each unit from step 5 as shown. Press the seam allowances in the direction indicated. The unit should measure 6½" square. Make 100 units.

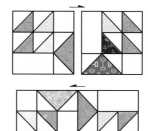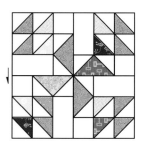

Make 100.

7 Lay out four units from step 6 in a four-patch arrangement, rotating the units as shown. Sew the units together in rows. Press the seam allowances in opposite directions from row to row. Join the rows and press the seam allowances in one direction. The block should measure 12½" square. Make a total of 25 blocks.

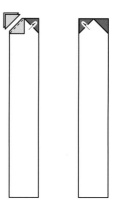

Make 25.

Making the Pieced Sashing

1 Sew a raspberry 1½" square to both corners at one end of a white 2½" x 12½" rectangle to make a *single* pieced-sashing unit. Make a total of 16 units.

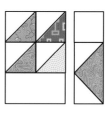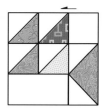

Make 16.

2 Sew a raspberry 1½" square to each corner of a white 2½" x 12½" rectangle as shown to make a *double* pieced-sashing unit. Make a total of 24 units.

Make 24.

Assembling the Quilt Top

1 Lay out the blocks, pieced-sashing units, and raspberry 2½" squares as shown in the quilt assembly diagram below, making sure to orient the pieced-sashing units as shown. The triangle corners should make small stars when the strips are positioned correctly. Once you're satisfied with the arrangement, sew the pieces together into rows. Press the seam allowances toward the pieced-sashing units.

2 Join the rows and press the seam allowances toward the sashing rows. The quilt top should measure 68½" square.

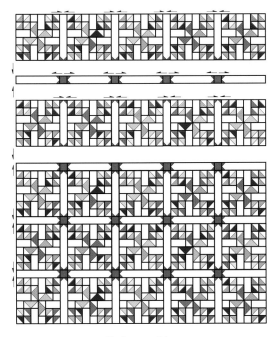

Quilt assembly

3 Join the raspberry 1½"-wide strips end to end to make a long strip. Referring to "Adding Borders" on page 9, measure and cut the inner-border strips, and then sew them to the quilt top. Press the seam allowances toward the inner border.

4 Repeat to add the multicolored outer-border strips to the quilt top. Press the seam allowances toward the outer border.

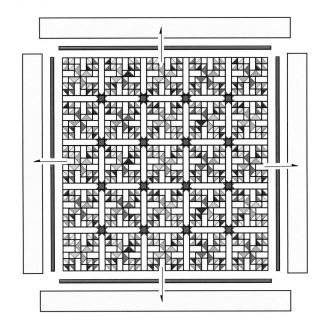

Finishing the Quilt

For detailed instructions, refer to "Quiltmaking Basics" on page 7.

1 Layer the quilt top, batting, and backing; baste the layers together. Quilt as desired.

2 Referring to "Binding" on page 9, use the raspberry 2½"-wide strips to bind your quilt.

A "Digital" Trip around the World

The small 2" squares remind me of the bits and bytes of our digital world scrambled about, yet so organized in their information delivery.

Materials

Yardage is based on 42"-wide fabric unless otherwise noted.

40 squares, 9" x 9", of bright prints for center block and borders*

1¾ yards of white solid for borders

2 yards of navy print for outer border and binding

4½ yards of fabric for backing

78" x 78" piece of batting

You can use the leftover fabrics from "Summer Time" on page 54.

Cutting

From the assorted bright squares, cut *a total of*:

352 squares, 2½" x 2½"

From the *lengthwise grain* of the white solid, cut:

2 strips, 4½" x 56½"

2 strips, 4½" x 48½"

2 strips, 4½" x 40½"

2 strips, 4½" x 32½"

2 strips, 4½" x 24½"

2 strips, 4½" x 16½"

From the *lengthwise grain* of the navy print, cut:

2 strips, 6½" x 60"

2 strips, 6½" x 72"

4 strips, 2½" x 72"

Making the Center Block

1 Sew four bright 2½" squares together to make a Four Patch block. Press the seam allowances in the directions indicated. The block should measure 4½" square. Make a total of 88 blocks.

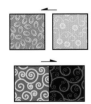

Make 88.

2 Lay out 16 Four Patch blocks in four rows of four blocks each as shown. Sew the blocks together into rows. Press the seam allowances in opposite directions

Designed and pieced by Gerri Robinson.
Machine quilted by Rebecca Segura.

FINISHED QUILT: 68½" x 68½"

FINISHED BLOCK: 4" x 4"

from row to row. Join the rows and press the seam allowances in one direction. The center block should measure 16½" square.

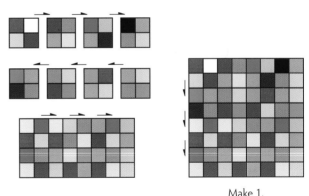

Make 1.

Making the Pieced Borders

1 Sew six Four Patch blocks together to make a border strip. Press the seam allowances in one direction. The strip should measure 4½" x 24½". Make two strips.

Make 2.

2 Sew eight Four Patch blocks together to make a border strip. Press the seam allowances in one direction. The strip should measure 4½" x 32½". Make two strips.

Make 2.

3 Sew 10 Four Patch blocks together to make a border strip. Press the seam allowances in one direction. The strip should measure 4½" x 40½". Make two strips.

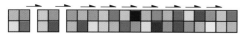

Make 2.

4 Sew 12 Four Patch blocks together to make a border strip. Press the seam allowances in one direction. The strip should measure 4½" x 48½". Make two strips.

Make 2.

Assembling the Quilt Top

1 Sew the white 16½"-long strips to opposite sides of the center block. Press the seam allowances toward the white strips. Sew the 24½"-long strips to the remaining two sides of the block. Press the seam allowances toward the white strips. The quilt center should measure 24½" square.

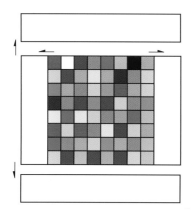

2 Sew the 24½"-long pieced border strips to opposite sides of the quilt center. Press the seam allowances toward the white strips. Then sew the 32½"-long pieced border strips to the two remaining sides and press the seam allowances toward the white strips. Repeat to sew

the remaining borders to the quilt center as shown in the quilt assembly diagram. Once all of the borders are added the quilt top should measure 56½" square.

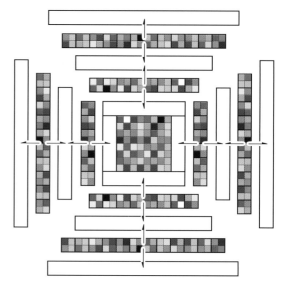

Quilt assembly

3 Referring to "Adding Borders" on page 9, measure and cut the navy 6½"-wide strips; then sew them to the quilt top for the outer border. Press the seam allowances toward the outer border.

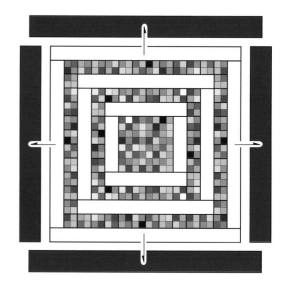

Finishing the Quilt

For detailed instructions, refer to "Quiltmaking Basics" on page 7.

1 Layer the quilt top, batting, and backing; baste the layers together. Quilt as desired.

2 Referring to "Binding" on page 9, use the navy 2½"-wide strips to bind your quilt.

Fat Quarters

Fat quarters are the true cornerstone of precuts. They've been tried and tested over the years and continually deliver the right amount of fabric to create some amazing and incredible quilts.

Rugby Stars

"Rugby Stars" was inspired by the classic rugby stripe of the '70s—strong horizontal rows creating a very distinct and iconic striped pattern.

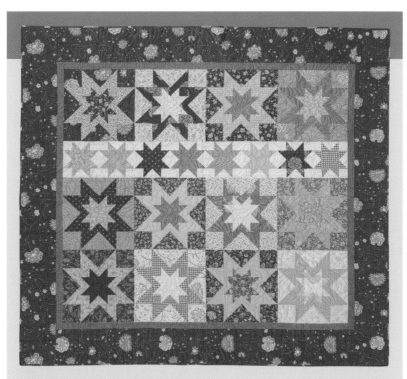

Designed and pieced by Gerri Robinson.
Machine quilted by Rebecca Segura.

FINISHED QUILT: 84½" x 76½"
FINISHED BLOCKS: 16" x 16" and 8" x 8"

Materials

Yardage is based on 42"-wide fabric unless otherwise noted. Fat quarters measure 18" x 21".

12 fat quarters of assorted red prints for blocks
12 fat quarters of assorted cream and tan prints
    for blocks
½ yard of cream solid for small Star blocks
⅔ yard of blue solid for inner border
3⅛ yards of red print for outer border and binding
7½ yards of fabric for backing
86" x 94" piece of batting

Cutting

A different set of red, cream, and/or tan fabrics is used for each large Star block. Before cutting, determine the placement of the fabrics in each large Star block. Cut the pieces for all the large Star blocks before cutting the pieces for the small Star blocks. The small Star blocks are cut from the remainder of the fat quarters. Repeat the cutting directions to make 12 large Star blocks and 8 small Star blocks, keeping the fabrics for each block separate.

For One Large Star Block

From the assorted red, cream, and tan fat quarters, cut:
1 square, 4½" x 4½" (center star)
8 squares, 2½" x 2½" (center star)
8 squares, 4½" x 4½" (outer star)
4 rectangles, 2½" x 4½" (outer star)
4 squares, 2½" x 2½" (outer star)
4 rectangles, 4½" x 8½" (background)
4 squares, 4½" x 4½" (background)

For One Small Star Block

From the remaining assorted red, cream, and tan fat quarters, cut:
1 square, 4½" x 4½"
8 squares, 2½" x 2½"

For Small Star Background

From the cream solid, cut:
32 rectangles, 2½" x 4½"
32 squares, 2½" x 2½"

Continued on page 64.

For Borders and Binding

From the blue solid, cut:

7 strips, 2½" x 42"

From the *lengthwise grain* of the red print, cut:

2 strips, 8½" x 73"
2 strips, 8½" x 80"

From the remaining red print, cut:

9 strips, 2½" x 42"

TECHNIQUE USED

• Flying-Geese Units (page 7)

Making the Large Star Blocks

Instructions are for making one block, using the pieces cut for one large Star block.

1 Use two matching center-star 2½" squares and one outer-star 2½" x 4½" rectangle to make a flying-geese unit. Make four matching units.

Make 4.

2 Sew flying-geese units from step 1 to opposite sides of a matching center-star 4½" square. Press the seam allowances toward the center. The unit should measure 4½" x 8½".

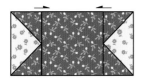

Make 1.

3 Sew matching outer-star 2½" squares to both ends of each remaining flying-geese unit to make two 2½" x 8½" strips. Press the seam allowances toward the cream squares.

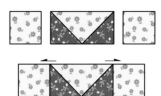

Make 2.

4 Sew the strips from step 3 to the center unit from step 2 as shown. Press the seam allowances toward the center. The star unit should measure 8½" square.

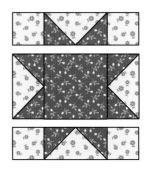

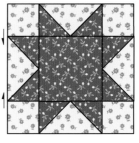

Make 1.

5 Sew two matching outer-star 4½" squares and one background 4½" x 8½" rectangle together to make a large flying-geese unit. Make four matching units. If desired, set aside the trimmed triangles to use for "Board Game" on page 67.

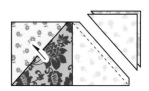

Make 4.

6 Sew two flying-geese units from step 5 to opposite sides of the star unit from step 4 to make a center unit. Press the seam allowances toward the star unit. The unit should measure 8½" x 16½".

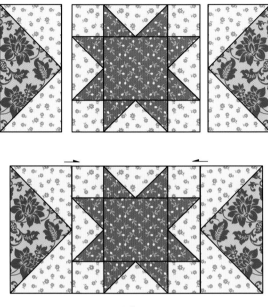

Make 1.

7 Sew background 4½" squares to both ends of the remaining flying-geese units to make two 4½" x 16½" strips. Press the seam allowances toward the background squares.

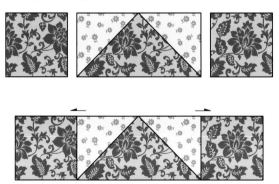

Make 2.

8 Sew the strips from step 7 to the unit from step 6 to complete the large Star block. Press the seam allowances toward the center. The block should measure 16½" square. Repeat to make a total of 12 blocks.

Make 12.

Making the Small Star Blocks

Instructions are for making one block, using the pieces cut for one small Star block and the cream background pieces.

1 Use two matching small-star 2½" squares and one cream 2½" x 4½" rectangle to make a flying-geese unit. The unit should measure 2½" x 4½". Make four matching units.

Make 4.

2 Sew two flying-geese units from step 1 to opposite sides of a matching small-star 4½" square to make a center unit. Press the seam allowances toward the center. The unit should measure 4½" x 8½".

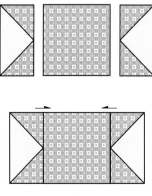

Make 1.

3 Sew cream 2½" squares to both ends of the remaining flying-geese units to make two 2½" x 8½" strips. Press the seam allowances toward the cream squares.

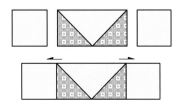

Make 2.

4 Sew two strips from step 3 and one center unit from step 2 together to complete a small Star block. Press the seam allowances toward the center. The block should measure 8½" square. Repeat to make a total of eight blocks.

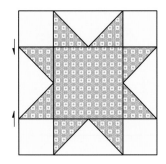

Make 8.

Assembling the Quilt Top

1 Sew four large Star blocks together to make a row. Press the seam allowances in one direction. The row should measure 16½" x 64½". Make three rows.

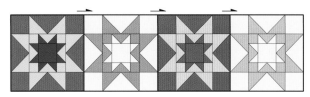

Make 3.

2 Sew the small Star blocks together to make a row. Press the seam allowances in one direction. The row should measure 8½" x 64½".

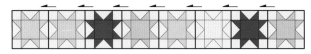

Make 1.

3 Lay out the rows from steps 1 and 2 as shown in the quilt assembly diagram below. Join the rows to complete the quilt center. Press the seam allowances in one direction. The quilt center should measure 64½" x 56½".

4 Join the blue 2½"-wide strips end to end to make a long strip. Referring to "Adding Borders" on page 9, measure and cut the inner-border strips; then sew them to the quilt top. Press the seam allowances toward the inner border.

5 Repeat to add the red 8½"-wide outer-border strips. Press the seam allowances toward the outer border.

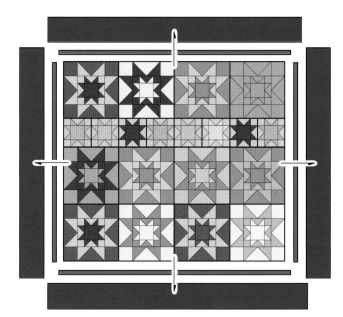

Quilt assembly

Finishing the Quilt

For detailed instructions, refer to "Quiltmaking Basics" on page 7.

1 Layer the quilt top, batting, and backing; baste the layers together. Quilt as desired.

2 Referring to "Binding" on page 9, use the red 2½"-wide strips to bind your quilt.

Board Game

The "Board Game" design is reminiscent of an antique Parcheesi game.

Materials

Yardage is based on 42"-wide fabric unless otherwise noted.

1½ yards of red floral for border and binding

64 half-square triangles of assorted red prints for blocks*

64 half-square triangles of assorted cream and tan prints for blocks*

⅞ yard of cream solid for blocks and sashing

½ yard of red solid for blocks and sashing

3½ yards of backing fabric

59" x 59" piece of batting

You can use the leftover half-square triangles from "Rugby Stars" on page 62. If you don't have any leftover triangles, you'll need 32 red squares, 4" x 4", and 32 cream and tan squares, 4" x 4". Cut the squares in half diagonally to yield 128 triangles.

Cutting

From the cream solid, cut

13 strips, 1½" x 42"

64 rectangles, 1½" x 3½"

From the red solid, cut:

8 strips, 1½" x 42"

16 squares, 1½" x 1½"

From the *lengthwise grain* of the red floral, cut:

2 strips, 6½" x 53"

2 strips, 6½" x 41"

4 strips, 2½" x 53"

Making the Blocks

1 To piece the triangles, sew a red triangle to the long side of each cream and tan triangle to make 64 half-square-triangle units. Press the seam allowances toward the red triangle. Trim the units to measure 3½" square.

Make 64.

2 Lay out four matching half-square-triangle units, four cream rectangles, and one red square as shown. Sew the pieces together into rows. Press the seam allowances toward the cream rectangles. Join the rows to complete the block. Press the seam

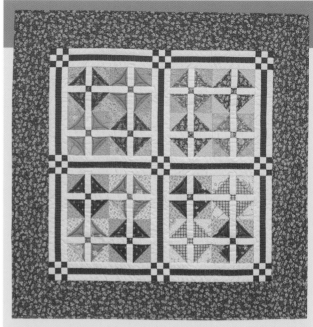

Designed and pieced by Gerri Robinson.
Machine quilted by Rebecca Segura.

FINISHED QUILT: 49½" x 49½"
FINISHED BLOCK: 14" x 14"

allowances toward the center. The block should measure 7½" square. Make a total of 16 blocks.

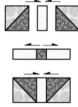

Make 16.

3 Sew four blocks from step 2 together to complete the larger block. Press the seam allowances in the directions indicated. The block should measure 14½" square. Make four of these blocks.

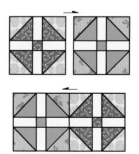 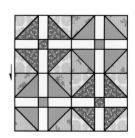

Make 4.

Making the Sashing

1 Sew a cream strip to each long side of a red strip to make a strip set. Press the seam allowances toward the red strip. Make six strip sets. Crosscut the strip sets into 12 sashing strips, 14½" wide. Crosscut the remainder of the strip sets into nine segments, 1½" wide.

Make 6 strip sets.
Cut 12 segments, 14½" wide,
and 9 segments, 1½" wide.

2 Sew a red strip to each long side of a cream strip to make a strip set. Press the seam allowances toward the red strips. Crosscut the strip set into 18 segments, 1½" wide.

Make 1 strip set.
Cut 18 segments, 1½" wide.

3 Arrange the segments from steps 1 and 2 in Nine Patch blocks as shown. Sew the segments together and press the seam allowances away from the center. The block should measure 3½" square. Make a total of nine blocks.

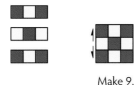

Make 9.

Assembling the Quilt Top

1 Lay out the blocks, the 14½"-wide sashing strips, and the Nine Patch blocks as shown. Sew the pieces together into rows. Press the seam allowances toward the sashing strips. Sew the rows together and press the seam allowances toward the sashing rows. The quilt

center should measure 37½" square.

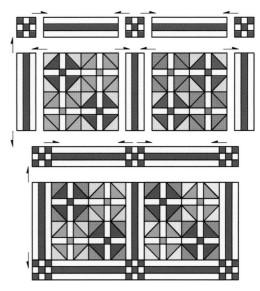

Quilt assembly

2 Referring to "Adding Borders" on page 9, measure and cut the red-floral 6½"-wide outer-border strips; sew them to the quilt top. Press the seam allowances toward the outer border.

Finishing the Quilt

For detailed instructions, refer to "Quiltmaking Basics" on page 7.

1 Layer the quilt top, batting, and backing; baste the layers together. Quilt as desired.

2 Referring to "Binding" on page 9, use the red-floral 2½"-wide strips to bind your quilt.

Board Game Pillow

Extra blocks from "Board Game" on page 67 can be used to create these box-style pillows.

Materials

Yardage is based on 42"-wide fabric unless otherwise noted.

16 half-square triangles of assorted red prints for blocks*
16 half-square triangles of assorted cream and tan prints for blocks*
½ yard of cream solid for blocks, sashing, and piping
¼ yard of red floral for border
1 square, 5" x 5", of red solid for blocks and sashing squares
⅞ yard of red fabric for pillow backing
21" x 21" square of muslin for pillow lining
21" x 21" square of batting for pillow
2¼ yards of ¼"-diameter cotton cording for piping
8 cream buttons, ¾" diameter
19" x 19" pillow form or polyester fiberfill

You can use leftover half-square triangles from "Rugby Stars" on page 62. If you don't have any leftover triangles, you'll need 8 red squares, 4" x 4", and 8 cream and tan squares, 4" x 4". Cut the squares in half diagonally to yield 32 triangles.

Cutting

From the cream solid, cut
24 rectangles, 1½" x 3½"
2"-wide bias strips to total 155"

From the red solid, cut:
9 squares, 1½" x 1½"

From the red floral, cut:
2 strips, 2½" x 15½"
2 strips, 2½" x 19½"

From the red fabric for pillow backing, cut:
1 square, 19½" x 19½"
2 strips, 4" x 38½"

Making the Pillow Top

For detailed illustrations on the following techniques refer to "Making the Blocks" on page 68.

1 To piece the triangles, sew a red triangle to the long side of each cream triangle to make 16 half-square-triangle units. Press the seam allowances toward the red triangle. Trim the units to measure 3½" square.

2 Lay out four matching half-square-triangle units, four cream rectangles, and one red square as shown in step 2 on page 68. Sew the pieces together into rows. Press the seam allowances toward the cream rectangles.

Designed and pieced by Gerri Robinson. Made by Patty Lanum.

FINISHED PILLOW: 19" x 19"
FINISHED BLOCK: 7" x 7"

Join the rows to complete the block. Press the seam allowances toward the center. The block should measure 7½" square. Make a total of four blocks.

3 Sew cream rectangles to opposite sides of a red square to make a sashing strip. Press the seam allowances toward the cream rectangle. Make four.

Make 4.

4 Lay out the four blocks, four sashing strips, and the remaining red square as shown. Sew the pieces together in rows. Press the seam allowances toward the sashing strips. Join the rows and press the seam allowances toward the center. The pillow top center should measure 15½" square.

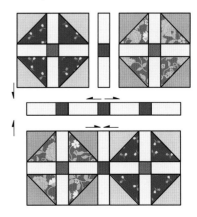

5 Sew the red-floral 15½"-long strips to opposite sides of the pillow top center. Press the seam allowances toward the border. Sew the 19½"-long strips to the remaining two sides to complete the pillow top. Press the seam allowances toward the border.

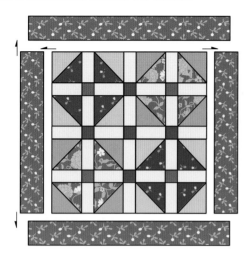

Finishing the Pillow

For detailed illustrations on the following techniques refer to "Finishing the Cushion" on page 48.

1 Layer the pillow top with the batting and the 21" square of muslin. Baste the layers together. Quilt as desired.

2 Trim the backing and batting even with the edges of the pillow top. Machine baste around the block about ⅛" from the outer edges.

3 Sew the cream bias strips together to make a continuous strip. Use this strip to cover the cording and make the piping as described in "Covered Cording" on page 49. Trim the seam allowances evenly to ¼".

4 Align the raw edges of the pillow top and piping. Sew the piping around the edge of the pillow top with a ¼" seam allowance. Start in the middle of the bottom edge and stitch around the pillow, overlapping the beginning and ending tails of the piping. Stitch across the piping where the tails cross, as shown on page 48. Trim the ends of the piping even with the raw edge of the pillow top.

5 Repeat step 4 to sew the piping around the edge of the red 19½" square to make the pillow bottom.

6 Join the short ends of the red 4"-wide strips to make a continuous loop for the boxing strip. Fold the strip into quarters and lightly press to mark the corner placement, making sure the seam lines are *not* in a corner.

7 Arrange the boxing strip on the pillow top, right sides together with the raw edged aligned; place a creased lined in each corner. Sew the strip to the pillow top, stitching all around the square and stopping where you started with a backstitch. When you reach a corner, stop in the exact corner with the needle in the down position. Clip the strip almost to the needle to spread the strip around the corner. Pivot the pillow top and continue sewing, clipping each corner as you come to it.

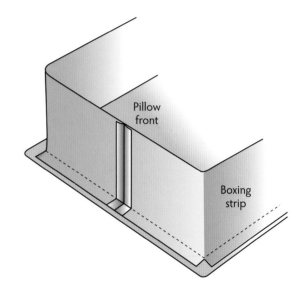

Pillow front

Boxing strip

8 Sew the boxing strip to the pillow bottom in the same way, stopping with a backstitch about 6" from where you started. Turn the pillow right side out.

9 Insert the pillow form or firmly stuff the pillow with polyester fiberfil. Turn under the ¼" seam allowance along the opening and stitch the opening close.

10 Referring to the photo on page 71 for placement guidance, mark the position of the buttons on the pillow bottom. Thread a needle with about a 24" length of thread and knot both ends. On one of the marks, insert the needle into the pillow bottom and bring it up to the pillow top, pulling the thread through to the knot. Insert the needle through a button hole and down again through the second hole. Insert the needle back through the pillow to the bottom and add a button to the pillow bottom. Pull the thread very tight to create the tuft in the pillow. Continue sewing, making several more stitches to firmly attach the button to the pillow. Knot the thread on the back and clip the thread.

11 Repeat step 10 to add the remaining buttons as shown in the photo.

Moonlight

Twinkling stars dancing across this quilt's Log Cabin–style background make me think of a clear night when stars and moonlight illuminate the homes below.

Designed and pieced by Gerri Robinson.
Machine quilted by Rebecca Segura.

FINISHED QUILT: 78½" x 78½" **FINISHED BLOCK:** 8" x 8"

Materials

Yardage is based on 42"-wide fabric unless otherwise noted. Fat quarters measure 18" x 21".

21 fat quarters of assorted tan prints for blocks
    and sashing
2⅞ yards of cream solid for blocks and sashing
¾ yard of dark-tan print for binding
7¾ yards of fabric for backing
88" x 88" piece of batting

Cutting

From the cream solid, cut:
28 squares, 4½" x 4½"
405 squares, 2½" x 2½"
104 squares, 1½" x 1½"

From the assorted tan prints, cut *a total of:*
8 rectangles, 2½" x 18½"
4 rectangles, 2½" x 10½"
92 rectangles, 2½" x 8½"
72 rectangles, 2½" x 6½"
184 rectangles, 2½" x 4½"
184 squares, 2½" x 2½"

From the dark-tan print, cut:
9 strips, 2½" x 42"

TECHNIQUES USED

• Flying-Geese Units (page 7)
• Pieced Sashing (page 8)

Making the Chain Blocks

1 Sew two cream 2½" squares and two tan squares together to make a four-patch unit. Press the seam allowances in the directions indicated. The unit should measure 4½" square. Make a total of 36 units.

Make 36.

2 Sew tan 2½" x 4½" rectangles to opposite sides of a four-patch unit to make a center unit. Press the seam allowances toward the tan rectangles. The unit should measure 4½" x 8½". Make 36.

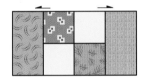

Make 36.

3 Sew a cream 2½" square to one end of a tan 2½" x 6½" rectangle to make a 2½" x 8½" strip. Press the seam allowances toward the tan rectangle. Make 72.

Make 72.

4 Sew two pieced strips from step 3 and one center unit from step 2 together to complete a Chain block. Press the seam allowances toward the pieced strips. The block should measure 8½" square. Make a total of 36 blocks.

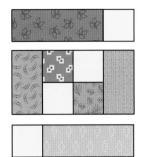

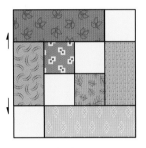

Make 36.

Making the Star Blocks

1 Use two cream 2½" squares and one tan 2½" x 4½" rectangle to make a flying-geese unit. The unit should measure 2½" x 4½". Make a total of 112 units.

Make 112.

2 Sew two flying-geese units from step 1 to opposite sides of a cream 4½" square as shown to make a center unit. Press the seam allowances toward the center. The unit should measure 4½" x 8½". Make a total of 28 units.

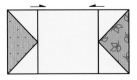

Make 28.

3 Sew a tan square to each end of the remaining flying-geese units to make 2½" x 8½" strips. Press the seam allowances toward the tan squares. Make a total of 56 strips.

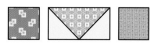

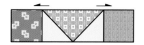

Make 56.

4 Sew two pieced strips from step 3 and one center unit from step 2 together to complete a Star block. Press the seam allowances toward the center. The block should measure 8½" square. Make a total of 28 blocks.

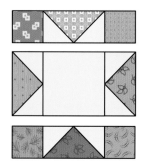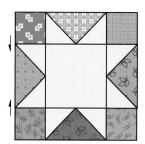

Make 28.

Assembling the Quilt Top Center

1 Sew a cream 1½" square to each corner on one end of a tan 2½" x 8½" rectangle to make a pieced-sashing unit. The unit should measure 2½" x 8½". Make 52 units.

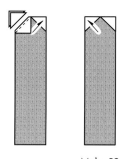

Make 52.

2 Lay out the Chain blocks, pieced-sashing units, tan 2½" x 8½" rectangles, and cream 2½" squares as shown in the quilt assembly diagram below, making sure to orient the pieced-sashing units as shown. The triangle corners should make small stars when the strips are positioned correctly. Once you're satisfied with the arrangement, sew the pieces together into rows. Press the seam allowances toward the pieced-sashing units.

3 Join the rows and press the seam allowances in the direction indicated. The quilt top should measure 58½" square.

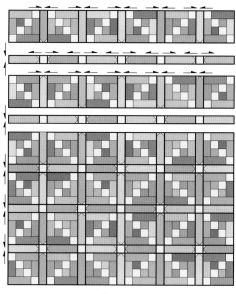

Quilt assembly

Adding the Borders

1 Lay out two tan 2½" x 8½" rectangles, two tan 2½" x 18½" rectangles, and three cream squares as shown. Sew the pieces together to make the top inner-border strip. Press the seam allowances toward the tan rectangles. The strip should measure 2½" x 58½". Repeat to make the bottom inner-border strip.

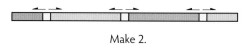

Make 2.

2 Lay out two tan 2½" x 10½" rectangles, two tan 2½" x 18½" rectangles, and three cream squares as shown. Sew the pieces together to make a side inner-border strip. Press the seam allowances toward the tan rectangles. The strip should measure 2½" x 62½". Repeat to make a second side inner-border strip.

Make 2.

3 For the outer border, sew six Star blocks and seven tan 2½" x 8½" rectangles together as shown to make the top border. Press the seam allowances toward the tan rectangles. The strip should measure 8½" x 62½". Repeat to make the bottom border.

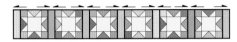

Top/bottom border
Make 2.

4 Sew eight Star blocks and seven tan 2½" x 8½" rectangles together as shown to make a side border. Press the seam allowances toward the tan rectangles. The strip should measure 8½" x 78½". Repeat to make a second side border.

Side border
Make 2.

5 Sew the top and bottom inner-border strips to the quilt center, and then sew the side inner-border strips to the quilt center. Press all the seam allowances toward the inner border.

6 Sew the top, bottom, and side outer-border strips to the quilt top. Press all seam allowances toward the inner border.

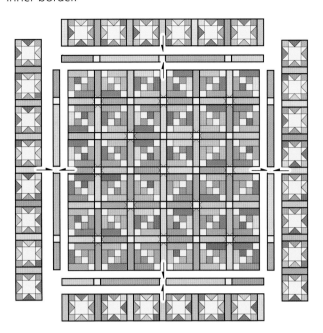

Finishing the Quilt

For detailed instructions, refer to "Quiltmaking Basics" on page 7.

1 Layer the quilt top, batting, and backing; baste the layers together. Quilt as desired.

2 Referring to "Binding" on page 9, use the dark-tan 2½"-wide strips to bind your quilt.

Acknowledgments

A Cut Above would not have been possible without the incredible women who guided, supported, and helped me make it all happen.

First and foremost, Beth Hayes, editor of *McCall's Quilting* and *McCall's Quick Quilts Magazine.* Because of your strong belief in me and my work, you felt comfortable introducing me to the Martingale editorial staff. Thank you so much! You helped put this whole book concept in motion.

Mary Green, Karen Burns, and Karen Soltys, editorial staff of Martingale. Wow! Really? Seriously? Three words I continually repeated when we first met to discuss my initial book proposal and you walked me through the steps and requirements of writing a book for a publisher. I'm *wowed* by your endless support and direction and I *really* can't believe this dream has become a reality. *Seriously?*

Lissa Alexander, marketing director of Moda Fabrics. Where does one begin when it comes to Lissa? You're a magician! I'm not sure how you do it, but you get it all done; sometimes right before my eyes but most of the time, like a magician, with a wink and a wave of your hand. Thank you for believing in me and offering your support of my book concept and having all my numerous fabric requests magically appear on my doorstep. Thank you!

Rebecca Segura of Zeffie's Quilts, long-arm quilter extraordinaire and dear friend. I'm a true believer in the phrase "quilting makes the quilt," and quilting by Rebecca Segura makes my quilts sing. Thank you so much for your tireless support in getting my quilts quilted, quilt backs pieced, binding cut and stitched on, and turned around in record time. Yes, you do it all with a warm heart, beautiful smile, and contagious laugh. You truly are one-in-a-million! Thank you so much!

Patty Lanum of Custom Home Curtains. Thank you for always accepting my projects, no matter the timing or situation. Your home-decor knowledge and creativity adds that finishing designer touch to my pillows and accessories. Thank you!

Lisa Christensen of 3 Kids Designs. I know the things I ask you at times have you scratching your head, but I'm truly grateful for your unending willingness to go there with me. Your technical and computer-graphic skills continually amaze me and I'm so grateful you hung in there and helped me create a mock-up presentation book. The mock-up book served as my roadmap in developing *A Cut Above.* Thank you!

About the Author

Gerri Robinson lives in Dublin, Ohio, with her husband, Eric.

Gerri is the creative force behind Planted Seed Designs (www.plantedseeddesigns.com), an online retail store featuring her latest fabric designs, quilt patterns, and quilt kits. Her quilt designs are repeatedly featured in numerous national quilting magazines worldwide.

If you've followed Gerri for any length of time, you've come to realize her two favorite quilting blocks are Pinwheels and Stars. She loves the classic look of both and the movement they give a quilt.

Gerri's designs are not complicated. In fact, if you're comfortable making half-square-triangle units, flying-geese units, and quick-angled rectangles, there's no design you won't be able to master.

When Gerri is not involved with all things Planted Seed Designs, she's in the garden designing and expanding her garden beds or traveling to the West Coast to visit Josh, Andrew, and daughter-in-law, Andrea, or sitting in the football stands watching Michael play football for Butler University.